Why Me?

One Man's Journey Experiencing God's Undeserved Gifts and Love

MIKE MOUNTZ
with BOB RUHE

Cover photo by Rhoda Mountz.
All photos provided with permission, under extended license, or by the author.

Cover design by Leanne Coppola
Book design by Jamie Markle

Printed in the United States of America
Library of Congress Control Number: 2018959653

2 4 6 8 10 9 7 5 3 1 paperback

Visit us at MomosaPublishing.com

ISBN 978-1-7323016-3-4

This book is dedicated to the people who have loved me as I have loved them. They have inspired and encouraged me to write about the spiritual path my life has taken: Why Me? One Man's Journey Experiencing God's Undeserved Gifts and Love.

This book is lovingly dedicated to my wife, Rhoda, who is the most important person in my life, and to the memory of her daughters, Tara and Trisha. To my sons, Elton and Weston: I love you as much as any father could love his sons, and I am very proud of both of you. To my step-daughter, Tonya: I always wanted to have a daughter. I never dreamed that I would have one who I love as much as you. Thank you for all the love and support you have given me. No father could ever be prouder of his children than I am. I have enjoyed seeing that God is an important part of my children's lives. To my sister, Linda Mountz: Thank you for your love. To my parents, Elton and Lelia Mountz: I miss them deeply. I thank them for the wisdom, love, and guidance that they have given me. To my twelve grandchildren: You are the perfect example of God's grace.

Mike's wife, Rhoda

Mike is my husband, my best friend, my love, and my soul mate for life. I thank God for the blessing of Mike in my life every day.

Mike is a very special person. He is the kindest, fairest, most gentle, giving, sharing, and honest and open human being I have ever met. I feel this is why God chose to use him to write this book. He has touched so many lives in a very positive way, and I am thankful he has touched mine.

Thank you for being my husband, Mike. Thank you for sharing your experiences with the world. God has opened the doors for you to walk through, and you have made the journey. I love you to the moon and back, "millions and billions of times," as our grandson Braydon likes to say.

Love and prayers,
Rhoda Mountz

Contents

I. Introduction 11

II. Trust 19

III. The Journey Begins 33

IV. Driven to My Knees 39

V. Letting Go 43

VI. Greatest Love 57

VII. Needing Help 63

VIII. Answered Prayers 71

IX. Love and Loss 85

X. The Homeless 97

XI. Tests of Faith 117

XII. Carmelite Nuns 179

XIII. Feelings 225

XIV. Message 239

XV. Never-Ending Grace 247

XVI. Reflections 283

Final Thoughts 307

Acknowledgments 309

About the Author 311

About the Co-Writer 315

About the Co-Designer 317

In Memory 319

This book is about following your spiritual compass, and opening your heart and mind to the possibility of gifts and love beyond this world.

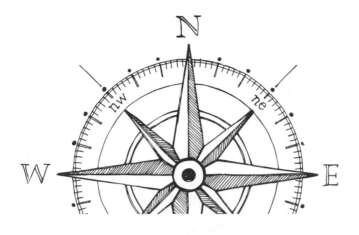

I.

Introduction

My name is Mike. I find it amazing that this book exists. I am a junior high school dropout who failed the second and third grades. I have never read a book except this book, and I am not someone who you would expect to write a book. But, here it is. I thank my co-writer and close friend Bob Ruhe for helping me to make this happen.

This book is about my spiritual experiences and the impact they have had on my life. I wrote this because many people encouraged me to share my experiences with others.

I struggle with reading and writing because I am severely dyslexic. I also suffer from bi-polar disorder. You will read more about how I have dealt with dyslexia in About the Author at the back of this book. I believe, however, that my difficulties with reading and writing have made me a good oral communicator, so I recorded my experiences to be transcribed into this book by Bob. Once my recorded text was written, Bob read it to me by phone, and we made alterations. I also sent him additional information or changes that I recorded on my iPad. This process continued until I was satisfied that we were finished with each section. I told Bob that I believe this book is why we met more than 40 years ago, and I believe that even more so now that the book is finished.

My references throughout this book to a compass pointing to true north reflect the belief I have that we are given a moral guidance system at birth. This is an instinct that points us in the right direction to being a good human being. It is part of how we understand the difference between right and wrong. This would be similar to the instinct a newborn lamb would have to get away from danger, even though it was never taught. The lamb just knows. The instinct was given to it at birth.

The concept comes from my experience using a compass so I would not get lost in the woods when I was hunting. When we get lost spiritually, this compass helps us to find our way to true north, our spiritual center. I believe the existence of this compass is an important part of how we find direction in our lives. I check if my compass is pointing true north by reviewing the Ten Commandments. I think what the Ten Commandments teaches us is worth while, regardless of what religion you follow.

The purpose of this book is to share Godly experiences that have occurred in my life. I feel very unworthy to have had these experiences. Many people I know are much more worthy than I. Nevertheless, I've come to the understanding, after speaking with many people, that my experiences are rare and unusual. Why they happened to me, I'm not sure.

I have sinned. I haven't always followed my compass. I have fallen short in living up to the teachings of the Bible and the voice of my own conscience, mostly because of sexual promiscuity in my past. I have followed the Ten Commandments, but I feel my sexual misconduct may have put me in a bad light in God's eyes. I am not without sin, and I ask for understanding and forgiveness.

Because I felt unworthy, I never thought my experiences were unusual. I would ask myself, *Doesn't this kind of thing happen to everybody? What do I have to say that would be of value and interest to anyone?* I thought it would be very egotistical of me to think I had anything to share, especially anything that would justify a book. I didn't plan to talk about my experiences, but conversations just seemed to happen. I did share them with my wife, Rhoda; my children Elton, Tonya, and Weston; and also with close friends; preachers I spent time with; and Carmelite nuns whom I consider friends and important spiritual leaders for me. I shared them truthfully and with a sense of awe and wonderment that they had happened to me. I was told these experiences had to be shared with more people, and it was these encouraging responses that helped lead me to this point. I have come to believe that my experiences are special and not something that happens to everyone. I am sharing them here so others can open their hearts and minds to the possibility of God's grace.

In addition to encouragement from family and friends, there was another reason I decided to write this book. One night, my hand and thoughts were guided to write the Grace Friendship and Partnership Contract. You'll read about this in Chapter XI, Tests of Faith. This occurred at my farm in Lancaster County, Pennsylvania, where Rhoda and I lived. A brilliant glow that was different than typical light moved toward me and then away from me at walking speed. It traveled a distance of 75 to 100 yards. This occurred two times. I was overcome with uncontrollable crying, and I knew that I was in the presence of God. After regaining my composure, I asked myself what I was going to do. Option one was to tell no one. I could keep it to myself as a private moment. This would be the safe thing to do. The experience was very intense, and I risked making a fool of myself, losing friends, losing credibility, and maybe even being locked up because people would think I had lost my mind. Option two was to share this experience, and the others I had, with as many people as I could. It took me a fraction of a second to decide that I was going to share these experiences with anyone who wanted to listen to or read about them.

I've asked God many times why these experiences occurred in my life. Was I chosen to challenge others to think about God's plans and the impact those plans could have on everyone's life? Was it to give people the opportunity to tell me I'm wrong and to open dialogue for other ways to interpret these experiences?

I am a visual person. I think in pictures. Perhaps that's why the image of a compass pointing to true north has been in my head for as long as I can remember. Yet I don't do the right thing all the time. No one does. I believe Jesus was probably the most perfect person ever to walk the earth. Was he without sin? I don't know, but his compass was pointed true north, and it's that compass that helps all of us find our way. The compass is why I believe we can all find God's grace, and the experiences I am about to share with you may help you find and follow your compass.

I can't picture life without these experiences. They have guided me through depression and dyslexia, which are profound problems I have dealt with throughout my life. They have opened my heart and mind to the possibility of God's presence and have given me peace and the confidence to think that way. They have led me to know that God can't be taken from me. Everything else can be taken away, but not God. I now live in New Zealand 90 percent of the year, and sometimes I get very lonely. I deeply miss my family and my friends, but God is always with me and that never changes. God can be with you too.

I call myself a Christian, but I think about and question the teachings of the Bible all the time. My beliefs may be no greater, or more valid, than yours. I could have been raised as a Muslim or a Jew. It just so happens that I am a Christian. A religious affiliation doesn't give people an inside track to God's grace.

I believe in the possibility of a life without sin or suffering. I believe a better world is available to us—a place like Heaven where rich and poor, black and white, and gay and straight can live in harmony.

This is possible if we make God the most important part of our lives.

I have never heard God's voice. I have never seen God and don't know what God looks like. But I have no doubt God is always present, whether we have sinned or not.

I don't profess to know God's intentions. I don't have a clue as to whether I am correctly interpreting the experiences I have had. I do, however, have a sense of what I should do. I believe I am charged with making others think beyond this world and themselves, and about the possibilities of God's grace—undeserved gifts and love.

I was blessed to be given the opportunity to experience things that have helped me find my way to God. Maybe you'll find your way too. Here are God's messages as I experienced them. I share them as honestly and as accurately as I can remember them, even when the experience is not something that I am proud of.

I hope you find my experiences thought-provoking. They are messages of hope that may challenge your thinking, whether you believe them or not.

Cheers,
Mike Mountz
Wanaka, New Zealand
and Lancaster County, Pennsylvania, 2018

There is no beginning or end to the universe, just as there is no beginning or end to God.

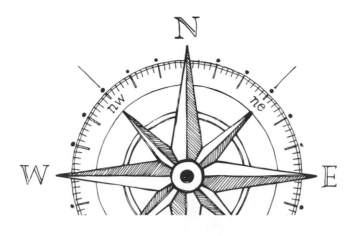

II.

Trust

Readers of this book may be curious about my religious beliefs. I do not believe all the doctrines of the church, and I believe there are many ways to interpret the teachings of the Bible. This has led me to formulate my own thoughts that I have had for most of my life. Along with these thoughts, I also have questions. You might find my thoughts and questions either enlightening, unsettling, or both.

I was not raised in a strong religious family. I don't recall my mother or father ever talking to me about God. There may have been a Bible in our house, but I don't remember seeing one. We did go to church occasionally, and I remember as a young boy how I would pass the time scribbling in the

Sunday program. I did think my grandmother was a spiritual person. She would make comments like "God is watching you," with a smile on her face and a twinkle in her eye. I know she had faith, which showed in her actions. I recall my Uncle Ralph coming home from the Army when I was around 10 years old and laying a pack of Marlboro cigarettes on the Bible in my grandmother's house. She went into orbit when he did this. She thought the Bible was sacred—not something to be treated disrespectfully. To this day I will not set something on a Bible. My Uncle George had been a pastor for a period of time, and my Uncle Jack was a missionary for a few years. I recall fondly that we would always have Thanksgiving dinner with my entire family in my grandmother's unfinished basement, and that one of my uncles would always say grace. There was spirituality around me, but it was nothing extraordinary, and I don't remember anyone ever talking to me about it. If they did, I just wasn't listening. Up until the time I went into the Army, my exposure to religion was probably very typical for someone my age.

I felt I was different when I was a pre-teen and a teenager. Maybe every kid thinks that way. I don't know. I just remember having special feelings inside. I looked at things, felt things, and was more sensitive to things than my friends, even if I didn't express those feelings. As I look back, I think those feelings were the seeds that blossomed into an awareness of God's presence. My first Godly experience occurred in the United States Army when I broke my hip. I had to lie perfectly still in a body cast for three months. That gave me a lot of time to think about God, my life, and if God was going to be a part of my life. I didn't understand my relationship with God yet. That would soon change. My hip healed without any sign that it had ever been broken. Doctors made comments to me about how unusual that was. As more of these experiences came along, my awareness turned into a deep belief in the existence of a God. You'll read more about my experience in the Army in this book.

I don't preach about these experiences. I don't believe I was ever intended to preach. I never seek out people to talk to about them. They just come up in the course of conversation, and people find them intriguing and thought-provoking. Preachers have told me I can talk to people they can't connect with because my style is so open and nonthreatening. I try to make people think about God. I am happy to have spirited conversations about religion and my Godly experiences, whether someone changes their thinking about God's grace or not.

There are many people in my life whom I would consider deeply spiritual in the way they live their lives and interpret the Bible. Many of these people are ministers, priests, or nuns. I am not like them, but I consider myself equally spiritual. We occasionally disagree on religious interpretation, but the discussion is always respectful of our various points of view.

What Do I Believe?

I believe deeply in the existence of a God. When I was young, I believed that God was a white male who lived in Heaven because that's how God was depicted in the religious images that I saw. I'm not sure about that now. I don't know if God is a man or a woman (I don't refer to God as he or him in this book), black or white, or simply an essence or superior source, something we can't see or touch. I don't know what God looks like; I just know that God is.

I believe God loves all of us, believers and non-believers, regardless of race, gender, religion, or sexual orientation. We are all equal in God's heart. I remind myself all the time not to judge others. Judging is best left to God.

I believe God created the universe and everything

within it. The scope of the universe is impossible to comprehend, but for it to exist, it had to be created. I don't believe the universe has a beginning or an end, and I feel the same way about God.

I call myself a Christian. That's a choice I have made, but I feel my choice is no better or more valid than any other religion. There is more than one way to think about God or to worship. I go to church and feel close to God when I'm there, but I feel close to God everywhere. I enjoy communion. I don't know if the bread, wine, or grape juice is the body and blood of Christ; I question that. I just know I feel close to God when I take communion. My friend Ned has reminded me that the true measure of being a Christian is to live with love, joy, peace, patience, kindness, goodness, gentleness, and self-control. I believe that, and I think of myself as a work in progress.

I love and believe in Jesus Christ. I believe Jesus walked the earth. I believe Jesus was sent to Earth through human birth as you and I were. I believe that he was a child of God, just as all of us are. I am not sure that Jesus was divine. I can accept it if he wasn't, but I do believe that Jesus was very special. I believe that Jesus did many miracles with the help of God. I believe that God spoke through Jesus. I believe that Jesus's faith was tested throughout his life. I believe that Jesus was crucified on the cross for his beliefs and for our sins. I believe that on the third day, Jesus was raised from the grave and taken to Heaven. I believe that we are all given the opportunity to go to Heaven through God's grace. I believe Jesus was God's most perfect child, who did God's work on Earth as he was asked. I believe that he was a light and a compass to show us the way to God's grace. I believe that God gave Jesus a purpose, and Jesus fulfilled that purpose. The impact of Jesus's presence has lasted for more than 2,000 years. I believe that God's presence has been since the beginning of time and will be forever. This is what I believe about Jesus. I respect that others believe that Jesus was God as the Christian Bible teaches.

I don't know if Jesus was without sin. We know very little about Jesus between the ages of 12 and 30. He may have sinned as we all do from time to time. Whether he sinned or not, he would have understood how temptation is a part of being human.

The world is filled with good people of different faiths who have sinned. I don't believe you must be a Christian to experience God's grace. I believe I will go to Heaven and will find it to be filled with people of different faiths and beliefs, people who have lived their lives in very different ways. I don't want to go there if the only people I find are

Christians. I want to be with all the children of God in the beauty and peace of Heaven.

I believe the world's great religions—Judaism, Islam, Christianity, Buddhism, Hinduism, and all religions—were given the teachings of one or many to follow. For Christians the teacher was Jesus.

I talked about my compass in the introduction. I believe this compass is given to us at birth, by God, and it's a force that guides us throughout our lives. As a Christian, I try to keep my compass pointing to true north by following the Ten Commandments.

1. You shall have no other gods before me.
2. You shall not make idols.
3. You shall not take the name of the Lord your God in vain.
4. Remember the Sabbath day, to keep it holy.
5. Honor your father and your mother.
6. You shall not murder.
7. You shall not commit adultery.
8. You shall not steal.
9. You shall not bear false witness against your neighbor.
10. You shall not covet.

I believe religion has done many good things and bad things throughout history. I know religion has started many wars. Many people have lost their lives over religion. I don't believe that God ever intended for that to occur.

I believe in the power of prayer. Every morning in the shower I start my day by praying and talking to God. I start my prayers by saying, "God, this is your son Michael. I hope and pray that you are doing well." I know I don't have to introduce myself to God, but I like to do it anyway. When I ask if God is doing well, I often wonder if God ever has a bad day. Introducing myself and asking how God is doing always make me smile. I think of praying as a conversation that I am having with my best friend—someone whom I love and who I know loves me. It is talking as much as it is praying. Prayer is what keeps God always with me.

Being in the shower and talking with God is a special time for me. I might stand, kneel, or sit on a bench that I had installed in the shower. I enjoy my shower because the warm water makes me feel like I am cleansing my body, and talking with God makes me feel like I am cleansing my soul. I ask God to help me handle all the problems and opportunities that will come my way. My talks with God may last from 5 to 10 minutes and occasionally longer. I pray for my family, my friends, and people who have had problems with me. I pray to give thanks for Rhoda, my children, and my grandchildren. I pray for people who have hurt me so that I can find the strength to keep them out of my "hate box," which is not easy to do. I pray for people whom I have hurt so they can find forgiveness in their hearts for me. I pray that I am doing things to the best of my ability, and that I am accurate and honest in what I say to others. I pray that the writing of this book is being guided by the thoughts of God and that I understand what God has asked me to do. I pray that this book is meaningful to people, and that it gives them enjoyment and an understanding of God's grace. I pray for the health of people I love when they are sick or hurt. I prayed for Rhoda after she had a very serious heart attack. She was healed, but if God had called her to Heaven, I would have accepted that as God's plan, even though it would have been the saddest day of my life. I end my morning talk with God with a prayer that serves as a road map for how I try to live my life. God will always be first in my life. I will always strive to keep what I pray for in this order of importance:

> *God, give me the courage, the strength, the wisdom, and the ability to be a good Christian, to be a good husband, to be a good father, and to be a good employer. In God's name I pray. Amen*

I try to pray during the day and at meals, but it's not the same as in the morning in the shower. In the morning, I take my time and feel deeply engaged in what I am saying to God. It's very personal. When I pray later in the day and at meals, I often feel that I am rushing or just going through the motions. I prefer to pray by myself, especially when I am alone with God and in the beauty of nature. I find that to be more beneficial and honest. Public prayer, like in church, is also important to me. I feel close to God when I am in church, but I don't think my prayers in church are more important or meaningful than when I am alone. Prayers with family are also very important to me. These prayers are very meaningful to me, and I believe it's very important for my children and grandchildren to participate in family prayer.

We can be taught the value of prayer, and we can be given suggestions on how to pray, but I don't believe that there is a right or wrong way to pray. I believe praying does not require fancy words or great speaking skills. Mostly, I pray to give thanks. I do sometimes pray for God's help, but only when I have reached a point where I can't resolve something on my own. As I said before, my praying is a conversation that I am having with my best friend.

I believe there are boxes where we collect feelings. I have a "love box." At the top of this box is my God. After God is my wife, then my children, my parents, and then everything else I love in that order of importance. There is also a "like box" and a "dislike box" with items stacked in order of intensity. Then there is the "hate box." There is only one level of hate. When you hate, you hate. Hate is not measured in degrees. If someone falls into my hate category, I try to move them into the dislike box as quickly as I can. I believe that anyone in the hate category only hurts me. I try my best not to hate. I try my best to forgive and forget. Forgiving is easier than forgetting, and it is in forgiveness that I find peace.

I believe we can all be better and do more. I could be a better father. My father was preoccupied with running a business, and he didn't find a good work-life balance. The apple didn't fall far from the tree. I have provided financially and materially for my family, but not as much as I should have emotionally or with my time. I could have found a better balance between work and my relationship with my family and my God. My boys Elton and Weston, from my first marriage, suffered because of this, and I ask for their understanding and forgiveness.

Finally, I believe we can do more by helping people in need. My mother told a story about my picking out a puppy when I was a child. She said, "I knew you would pick that one. You always help the one that needs the help the most." Look around for those who need help and do all that you can for them. The rewards from doing this are immense.

We must also help ourselves. I spent a lot of time throughout my life beating up on myself when I should have learned from my experiences, reset my compass, and moved on. Life is too short to dwell on things we cannot change. Ask God for forgiveness when you stray off course, learn from your lessons, and then move on quickly. Keep your spiritual compass pointing true north, and trust that God is guiding you in the right direction. Helping others and helping yourself is a sure path to God's grace.

Mike, age 17, 1969

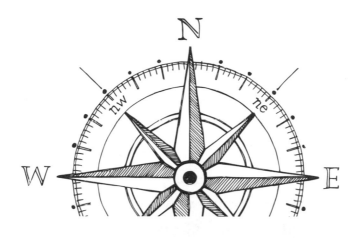

III.

The Journey Begins

I enlisted in the United States Army when I was 17 because a close friend of mine, Dennis Martin, dared me to join. Soon after the dare I enlisted. It wasn't the smartest thing I ever did to win a bet. Dennis and I often laugh about this and say to each other, "How crazy was that!"

I was stationed at Fort Dix, New Jersey. Soon after enlisting, my hips started to bother me, and I was put on a medical hold. During the first night I was on medical hold, I fell out of my five-foot-high upper-bunk bed and landed on my side. I didn't recall ever falling out of a bed before. The pain in my hips was excruciating, but no other part of my body was hurt, which I thought was strange because of the severity of the fall. I was taken to a local military hospital, where X-rays showed I had shattered my pelvis. I was put in a body cast from my armpits to my toes.

Two months later, I was strapped on a stretcher and transferred by helicopter to Valley Forge Military Hospital in Valley Forge, Pennsylvania. When I landed, a Red Cross volunteer ran to me and put a blanket over my body. This blanket had been knitted by a local woman as a gift for a soldier coming back from the Vietnam War. Soldiers who got these blankets were allowed to keep them. I cherish that blanket to this day. The volunteer asked me, "What limbs are you missing?" When I told her I wasn't missing any limbs, she started to cry. The hospital cared for thousands of soldiers who had lost arms or legs, and sometimes both, in the war. I guess she felt relief when she found out I was not an amputee. I was X-rayed while I was still in the body cast, and then cut out of my body cast so better X-rays could be taken to see if the breaks were healing properly. I'll never forget a doctor coming into the ward that included at least 40 other soldiers. He pulled a chair close to my bed and asked, "Why are you different?" He was smiling, but he had a quizzical, curious, almost shocked look on his face. "What do you mean, 'Why am I different?'" I asked.

The doctor showed me X-rays of my broken pelvis taken the day of the accident. It was very easy to see where the bones were broken. Then he showed me the X-rays they had just taken. My hips were perfect. There was no sign of them ever having been broken. "How does that happen?" the doctor asked incredulously. He explained that breaks in bones can be seen on x-rays for years after they heal. He had never seen X-rays where the bones healed so quickly without a trace of a break. I just shrugged my shoulders and could offer no explanation.

I recall wondering whether this was some kind of divine intervention. My bones had healed perfectly, and I wasn't going to Vietnam. Why was I spared, even though the reason I was spared was painful? I was in a body cast for months, and for the first time I gave serious thought to my relationship with God. I didn't yet understand the concept of God's grace. I didn't feel a calling to serve God, but I did think God played a role in what happened to me. Maybe there was a reason I couldn't recognize or understand at the time. It turns out, there was.

Over the years, I reflected more on my Army accident as other Godly experiences occurred in my life. I came to believe God had a plan. Being in a hospital with amputees was my window into the needs of veterans and how important it is to care for them and recognize them for the sacrifices they make. I had spent months lying perfectly still, and that gave me a lot of time to think. When I looked around and saw all those soldiers missing arms and legs, I understood how lucky I was. I vowed that if the opportunity ever came up to do something special for vets, I would. That opportunity came in 2003, when my business, Cloister Car Wash, founded Grace For Vets. By the end of 2017, the Grace For Vets organization had given more than 1.6 million free car washes to veterans and current service personnel in four countries. You can visit www.graceforvets.org to learn more about the program.

My Army accident made me aware of God's presence. It also made me aware of people's needs and the importance of saying thank you and giving back. These are qualities that lead us to God's grace. Grace For Vets has also given thousands of business people who joined the program the opportunity to say thank you, give back, and experience the joy of God's grace. I spoke with many of these car wash operators in 2010, when I was inducted into the International Car Wash Association Hall of Fame. You can listen to my induction speech by visiting YouTube under "Michael Mountz Car Wash Hall of Fame." I concluded my remarks by saying: "*Why did God put me in that hospital among soldiers who were missing their arms and legs? I was 17 years old and had simply fallen out of bed. Why was I there with those heroes? I believe God put me there so I could be here now, asking everyone in this audience to support our veterans. They deserve it."*

Today, I ask a similar question: Why am I writing this book when I have never read a book before writing *Why Me?* I believe in my heart that God wants me to do this to help others understand God's undeserved gifts and love. God truly does work in mysterious ways.

My accident in the military, the miraculous way my bones healed, my exposure to the amputees, and the inspiration to do something for veterans called me to open my heart and mind to God. I became much more aware of God's gifts. I believe God's grace is there for all of us if we are willing to accept God's presence. We are all the same. If we look, we will find. If we believe, we will receive. I kept looking, and many more experiences came to pass.

Actions have consequences that help us to learn.

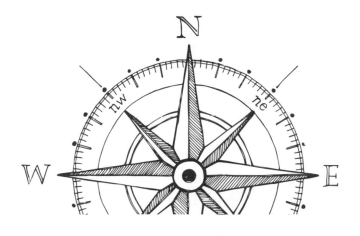

IV.

Driven to My Knees

My second Godly experience occurred when I was 19 years old. I was just out of the Army and had moved back to my parents' home in Morgantown, Pennsylvania. One night, I had sex with a married woman near to where I lived. This experience really forced me to think about the consequences of my actions.

I remember my walk home very clearly. I had a smile on my face, a bounce in my step, and I was so full of myself. There was a beautiful full moon illuminating my path. I felt great about what had just happened. It was a conquest and a real thrill for a 19-year-old. I was filled with bravado, pride, and cockiness. I felt no remorse or regret for what I had done, but that was about to quickly change.

As I approached my house, I reached the top of a small hill that overlooked our family home. Suddenly, I was driven to my knees, pushed down by some force that took total control of my body. There was no explanation for what knocked me down. I was in an open field, and I knew I didn't trip on anything. It happened so quickly that I didn't have time to be frightened. I instantly knew that I was receiving a strong message that my behavior was wrong and that I needed to think about what I had done.

This experience lasted for a few minutes. I didn't hear a voice speaking to me, and I can't say there was a voice in my head. It was as if thoughts were being poured into my brain by an outside force, challenging me to think about my indiscretion. There was no doubt in my mind that this was God making me aware that I should not put my personal pleasure first when that was the wrong thing for me to do and was hurtful to others. I was feeling good, and I shouldn't have been feeling good. I had broken one of the Ten Commandments by committing adultery. I did not follow my compass. I was learning that God is aware of the actions we take, right and wrong, in our lives.

I am thankful for the experience with the woman and the message that God sent me. I started to look for more of God's messages, and I found them everywhere. I became more aware of God's presence, and I started to think about the consequences of my actions, even if I didn't immediately change my ways. I believe this was all part of God's plan for me. I learned that if I was willing to open my heart and mind to God, I would be one step closer to God's wisdom, love, and forgiveness. I would be able to know and receive God's grace.

Mike at Cloister Car Wash in Reading, Pennsylvania, 2008

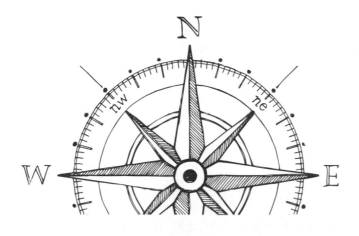

V.

Letting Go

I wanted to own and manage a business since I was in my early teens. My goal was to accomplish this by the time I was 30 years old. I grew up in my family's business, Morgan Trailer Manufacturing Company. By the time I was in my late twenties, I had worked my way up to an interesting and challenging job as head of Human Resources. I was well paid, drove a company car, and felt that I was good at my job. I enjoyed the work, especially working with people like Fran and Janet, but there was always something missing. Around this time, changes were occurring at Morgan. The company was in the midst of a serious business downturn. My father was stepping aside as

CEO, and my parents were in the middle of a bitter divorce. All of this forced me to think more seriously about what I was going to do. I never expected to take over the company, so I knew if I was going to accomplish my goal, I would have to find something that suited my interests and skills.

This was not an easy decision for me. I had been fighting with myself about this for years. I did have comfort and security with my job at Morgan. Other than serving in the Army and working on a farm and at a gas station when I was young, I had worked at Morgan all of my life. I was a high school dropout, and I felt my options were limited. I had two small children, a mortgage, and a family who depended on me to earn a living, but I was not pursuing my goal. Then one day when I was driving to work, I drove past my assigned parking spot and just kept driving. I was torn up inside, so much so that I developed a bleeding ulcer. I drove around trying to decide what to do with the rest of my life. I went to the local archery club and sat there for hours just praying and thinking. I never did go to work that day, and to my surprise, no one asked where I was or what I had been doing. That made me see how dispensable I was. I also realized I couldn't serve two masters. I couldn't look for a business with the intensity and commitment that was required, while at the same time giving 100 percent to Morgan. I decided I would resign and start looking for a company of my own.

When I turned in my letter of resignation, I was encouraged to rethink my decision, but I had made up my mind to resign. Even though I was the son of the founder of the company, I wasn't going to receive any special treatment. I did get back wages of a few hundred dollars that I was owed because I had deferred a wage increase during the business downturn. Because I resigned, I was not given severance pay. The company had recently given a severance package to another employee for circumstances that were similar to mine, but the same was not offered to me. That hurt. I was hoping for the money to help me and my family transition to a new work life. It was a lesson in the hard realities of business, but it fueled my desire to get working on my search for a company of my own. I had resigned, management accepted my decision, and it was time for me to move forward.

I felt like the weight of the world was on my shoulders. I had very little money saved, a few thousand dollars at the most, to support my family. I had walked away from a good job without an education to fall back on, and I had no immediate source of income. I had the support of my wife at the time, Patty, who was a teller at a bank, but I didn't know what I was going to do. I didn't even know how to go about finding a business, and I needed to earn money immediately. A friend of mine heard about my predicament and offered me a job cutting timber, which is extremely dangerous work. He taught me how to do the job well. I worked as a lumberjack, plus I did odd jobs as a carpenter, for two years. This was a good fit because I earned enough to pay the bills and had a flexible schedule that gave me time to look for a business.

I started my search for a business by looking in the newspaper, but I quickly found out that wasn't where I would find the kind of opportunity I was looking for. I had just turned 30 and found myself sitting in a chair in my living room getting down on myself because I hadn't reached the goal I set. I felt like a failure, and I started to second-guess my decision to leave Morgan. Then it dawned on me. I would be 30 for a year. I still had time to fulfill the age goal that I had set for myself. That re-energized me. I jumped up from the chair, and from that point I aggressively looked for a company to buy. I knocked on a lot of doors, and I told my story to every business owner who would see me. I looked at many financial statements to evaluate the numerous opportunities. These included a company that buried electric lines, a trailer park, an injection plastic molder, and many more, but none of them was a good fit for me. To be honest, I really didn't know exactly what I was looking for, but I was confident that when the right opportunity came along, I would know it.

Another year passed, and my wife had a party at our home to celebrate my 31st birthday. The kids went off to bed, and I found myself sitting alone in the same chair I had sat in a year earlier, thinking about how I had not met my goal of finding a business by the time I was 30. No one knew that I felt like a failure. I hadn't shared this with anyone. I remember feeling like the devil was on one shoulder telling me cutting timber was a business and everything was okay. On the other shoulder was an angel telling me cutting timber wasn't the type of business I wanted and that I should keep looking. I was in turmoil. Then I had an inspiration, and I knew exactly what to do. I would continue to look until I knew what God had planned for me. I would turn my search for a business over to God. It was just that simple. I said, "God, I'm putting this in your hands. If you want me to have a business, I'll have a business. If you don't want me to have a business, that's okay, too. I'll keep working hard at trying to find a business until you let me know your plans for me." This freed me from my turmoil. It lifted the weight of the world off of my shoulders. My predicament was now in God's hands. I "let go and let God." I recommitted myself to my search. If God's plan was for me to own a business, then that's what would happen. If not, then so be it. I had released myself into the hands of God, and when I did that, I had no more worries, and the pressure was gone.

My 31st birthday was December 22, 1984—the day I turned my search for a business over to God. On January 3, 1985, I received a phone call from a car wash owner in Ephrata, Pennsylvania. He told me that he had heard I was looking to buy a small business. He said that he might be interested in selling his car wash, and he wanted to know if I would like to see the facility. This happened 12 days after I decided to put my search in the hands of God. I subsequently bought the business on March 18, 1985, just 86 days after I put my dream of owning a business in God's hands.

You might think it was a coincidence that I got that phone call right after I put my fate in the hands of God. You might think it was just luck. However, I believe it was a Godly experience. I believe God was watching over me. Once I decided to believe in God's grace, the turmoil I had felt when searching for a business was over. Even if I had never found a business, my total trust in God relieved me of the burden I was carrying.

The name of the business was Cloister Car Wash. I now feel it was no coincidence that the name had spiritual connotations. The Cloister Foundation is located in Ephrata. It is the historical site of a religious sect that dates back to the 1700s. In 2006, I began a deep and spiritual friendship with the Carmelite nuns in Terre Haute, Indiana, a *cloistered* sect of the Catholic Church. You'll read more about my relationship with the nuns later in this book. At first, I didn't like the name "Cloister." I couldn't even spell "Cloister." I favored something easier to say and spell, like Mike's Car Wash, but I wisely decided not to change the name. I believe the name Cloister Car Wash was chosen by God; it was a part of God's plan for me. Keeping the name played a big role in the success the business enjoyed. I also felt God played a role in connecting me to a business that was perfectly suited to my skills and personality. I enjoyed marketing and promoting the company, the technical aspects of running the equipment and producing a high-quality product, and managing the finances. All of this came easily to me, even though I had no formal schooling. I was a risk taker by nature, and I also liked managing the risk. I had to borrow 100 percent of the money I needed to buy the business, and weather and business conditions were always putting a strain on cash flow. I then spent 28 years building a business that grew to four locations and won many industry and community awards. I am very proud of the fine reputation Cloister enjoyed locally, throughout the United States, and around the world. I can't think of another business or industry that would have been so perfectly suited to me.

Faith played a big role in my success. I had faith that when I turned my search for a business over to God, everything would work out. I had faith that if I found the right business, I would find the money to buy it. If I concentrated on having the money first, the right opportunity would have passed me by. I had faith in my ability to run the business when I had no prior experience running a car wash or any other type of business. I had faith that I would find and keep the right people to manage the operation. And, I had faith that the business would be successful and able to give back to the communities it served. All my faith came from my belief in God.

I had faith in God's help and guidance when I was searching for a business and on many other occasions throughout the 28 years I owned Cloister.

I expressed how important my faith in God was to me in our employee handbook. Thousands of these handbooks were given for free to prospective employees, new hires, and interested customers and vendors. Here's what was printed in the handbook:

The owner of this Company has a firm belief in God and desires to try to view all aspects of his life from a Christian perspective. Any comments or actions alluding to the Christian faith stem from a personal standpoint and are not intended to belittle any other religious beliefs or non-beliefs. All customers, vendors, and team members shall have the freedom to function in this Company regardless of their religious status. Religion will neither enhance nor hinder the possibility of advancement or service within the Company. As noted elsewhere in this Handbook, the Company does not discriminate on the basis of religion or religious beliefs.

I would turn to God for guidance when I had a troubling problem to solve. One good example of this occurred in 2005, when we were building our fourth car wash. This one was located in Reading,

Pennsylvania. The township supervisors told me that we did not have an acceptable process in place to handle rainwater runoff from extreme storms. The system they wanted installed involved elaborate underground piping that would have cost close to $1,000,000 to do. We had not budgeted for this expense, and we had already invested hundreds of thousands of dollars in the engineering and design. The cost was enough to shut down the project. This would have been devastating to my business. A few days after I learned about this problem, I was praying in the shower as I do every morning. I felt I couldn't handle the problem by myself. I didn't know what to do. Should I borrow more money or shut down the project? I once again turned to God for help and guidance, just like I did when I was searching for a business. The answer to the problem came to me in the middle of the next night. I woke up with what seemed like a crazy idea, but it was perfectly clear in my mind what to do. The solution was to install storage tanks in the ground instead of the piping. Even though the solution made sense to me, I didn't know if it would work. I went to my close friend, Ned Pelger, who was a consulting engineer on the project, and explained my idea and how it came to me. At first we didn't know if we could capture such a large amount of rainwater in tanks, and if we could, where would we find tanks big enough to do the job? We were also concerned that the cost of the tanks would be as prohibitive as the cost of the piping. After we determined the idea would work, we received approval from the township to proceed, but we had no idea where to get the tanks. Ned did some research, and miraculously we found four used 40,000-gallon beer tanks measuring 12 feet high by 44 feet long in North Carolina at a cost of $10,000 each, which was very inexpensive. They were perfect for what we needed. To add to our good fortune, we didn't encounter rocks when we dug the deep holes to bury the huge tanks. We had been using dynamite to break through rocks we were finding all around the property. When we didn't have to use dynamite to bury the tanks, we saved significant time and expense. God was truly watching over me and Cloister. The project was completed at a savings of close to $900,000 when compared to the piping design. I don't believe the idea to use the tanks would have come to me if I had not put my trust in God to find a solution.

Perseverance, hard work, and the help of a lot of wonderful, talented people made Cloister Car Wash successful. But there is no doubt in my mind that the single most important factor in my success was the day I put my search for a business in the hands of God. God's guiding hand led me to Cloister, which was the absolute perfect fit for me. Sometimes Godly experiences involve us helping others; sometimes God's guidance helps us. If you open your heart and mind to these possibilities, you too will experience God's undeserved gifts and love.

Mike and Rhoda were married on July 17, 1991, at a lake on the Allagash River in northern Maine during an eight-day, 100-mile canoe trip. A preacher brought the flowers. He landed on the lake in a pontoon plane at the halfway point of their trip to conduct the ceremony.

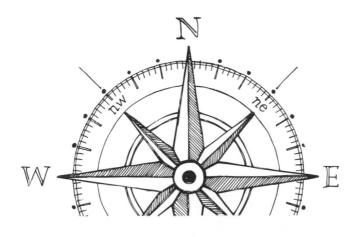

VI.

Greatest Love

I put God first in my life, but there is no person I have ever loved or will ever love like I love my wife, Rhoda.

One Sunday morning during the summer, I was eating breakfast by myself at a restaurant in Ephrata, Pennsylvania. I was sitting in the center of the main dining room, surrounded by tables and booths that were full of people. Thirty feet away from me there were two men and a woman sitting in a booth, talking and enjoying their breakfast. I didn't know them, and I didn't recall ever seeing them before. I looked at them for only a minute or two, and they didn't glance back at me. There was no particular reason for my eyes to be drawn to them. No one dropped a plate or spilled their coffee. They weren't loud or busy greeting people. I can't explain why, but my mind took a snapshot of these three people. One of them was going to become the most important part of my life after God.

Several years later, a woman who worked for me told me she had to leave because she was pregnant. She was responsible for planting and caring for the flowers that were always on display from spring to fall at the car wash. Her job was important and required some knowledge of plants and flowers, and I was disappointed that she would be leaving. I trusted her judgment and asked her if she knew anyone who would be capable and willing to take over her responsibilities. She said that her sister might be interested and that she would bring her to the car wash that night at 6 pm to meet me. When she and her sister Rhoda arrived, I was surprised to discover that Rhoda was the woman I had seen at the restaurant years earlier. I'm sure I startled her when I said, "You're the woman I saw years ago at the restaurant in Ephrata sitting with two men having breakfast!" The image of Rhoda sitting with those men in the restaurant was so clear that I could have painted a picture of it. It was burned into my mind with that kind of detail. I was surprised by my recollection of her, and I had the feeling that this was more than just a coincidence. It was like my mind took a photograph of her years earlier, filed it away undeveloped, and then instantly developed the photo when I was introduced to her. Rhoda agreed to take over for her sister, and that was the beginning of our life together.

The experience of my mind taking a snapshot of what seemed like a very normal moment has happened several times. Years later, someone from the snapshot is with me, and the image is brought to life. Sometimes these moments have been significant turning points in my life. That was certainly the case with Rhoda. I have always found this interesting, but I never thought of it as a Godly experience until it occurred with Rhoda and changed my life.

When Rhoda came into my life, I was married but had been separated for years. Rhoda and I kept our working relationship friendly and businesslike, but strong feelings for each other started to grow. Soon, we fell in love and decided to get married. Today, we have a wonderful blended family of children and grandchildren.

Rhoda has been my soulmate. I couldn't ask for anything more in my life than Rhoda and her daughter Tonya and my sons Elton and Weston.

Rhoda and I have shared many wonderful moments together, and she has been a spiritual guiding light through many of my Godly experiences.

I believe that the manner in which Rhoda came into my life was a Godly experience. I have met many people in unusual ways. Sometimes a meaningful friendship develops, but I think of these chance meetings as nothing more than good fortune. Meeting Rhoda was different. The impact she has had on me is profound, and the love we share is deeper than I can describe. I have always felt that God's hand brought us together.

I believe God knew that Rhoda and I needed each other. At first, God planted a memory in my mind, and then God brought that memory to life. My relationship with Rhoda and my love for her is the ultimate example of God's grace—God's undeserved gifts and love.

Early start! Mike, age 10, smoking a cigar

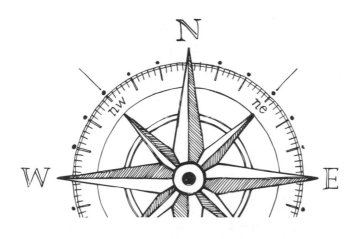

VII.

Needing Help

I probably first smoked as early as 10 years old, and I started to smoke regularly when I was 15. I was smoking as much as three packs of Marlboro cigarettes a day when I finally quit. I had tried to quit many times during the 25 years that I smoked. I would make a commitment to stop and then quit smoking for a while, but I always started again. I had tried a pipe and chewing tobacco to get away from cigarettes, but that didn't work. On New Year's Eve, December 31, 1990, my family was sitting around the kitchen table, and we all decided to make New Year's resolutions. That was something I had never done. When it was my turn to make a resolution, I said that I was going to stop smoking that coming year. Everybody started laughing because they knew I had tried over and over again to stop, and that I had always failed. To be honest, I felt that it was impossible, but I had made my resolution anyway with the hope that the resolution would commit me to make the real effort it would take to finally stop.

In June of 1991, I took my son Elton to Maine to go bear hunting. While we were on our hunt, I started thinking about my resolution and how I was still smoking. I said to myself over and over again, "I have to quit. It's six months into the year, and I'm still smoking." I thought about how I had tried to quit so many times, but I had always failed. One night when Elton and I were sitting in camp, I decided to do what I always did when I couldn't resolve a problem or a challenge on my own. I asked God for help. I prayed to God, "If you help me to stop smoking, I will stop smoking." By asking God for help, I created two choices for myself. One was I would stop smoking because I believed so strongly that when I asked God for help, God would help me. The other option was if I continued to smoke, I did not believe that God would help me. I knew immediately that I was going to stop smoking. I also knew it was not going to be easy, but I believed so deeply that God would help me that I knew I could do it.

The next day, the hunters in our camp were sitting in a van ready to travel to our hunting locations. I walked out of my cabin with an unopened carton of cigarettes under my arm. I walked over to an assistant guide and handed him the cigarettes. "What's this?" he asked. "They're for you," I said. "I am going to stop smoking!" I recall everyone in the van breaking up with laughter. I acknowledged their laughter with a smile, confident in my belief that God would give me the strength to finally quit.

I never smoked again.

I don't want to imply that when you ask God for help, your prayer is instantly and miraculously answered and your struggle is over. It wasn't easy to stop smoking. It was unbelievably tough. I would pray to God every time that I wanted to have a cigarette. This felt like I was having a continuous discussion for several weeks. I would have the feeling that I had overcome the urge to smoke, and then just like that, I would have an overwhelming desire to smoke again. I always thought that fighting this urge was a way of testing my faith and commitment. I didn't think of the challenge to stop smoking as overcoming nicotine withdrawal. I thought of it as a battle of good versus evil. My faith in God's help, guidance, and wisdom was the force of good, and the strong desire to smoke was evil. Every time I wanted a cigarette, I pictured Satan on my shoulder telling me it was okay to smoke. Every time my faith in God has been tested like this, I have kept my faith. I have never given up on my belief that God has a plan that would see me through a difficult time. Stopping smoking was another example of this. With God's help, anything is possible.

I think this was a Godly experience because I turned a difficult challenge that I faced over to God for help, and my prayer was answered. I don't ask for God's help casually. I believe God expects us to handle life's day-to-day challenges. However, there are challenges and problems that we are not strong enough to resolve without God's help and wisdom. "Ask, and you shall receive" is a profound truth stated in the Bible, but that doesn't happen unless you have deep faith in God's love and have made an effort on your own before you turn to God for help. I know I won't always get what I ask for, but I trust that God has a plan for me, even if I don't know what God's plan may be. We don't always receive what we ask for, but God is always listening to our prayers. I believe God will help all of us in times of need if our faith is sincere and we are deeply committed to changing something of great importance in our lives. When we have faith and the commitment to accomplish something, God's grace will shine upon us.

God helped me to stop smoking because I had reached a threshold—a point I couldn't get past by myself—in dealing with a problem. I wrestled with stopping smoking. I thought about it all the time. I had reached the point where I had to turn my problem over to God. When I did this, euphoria came over me. I was at peace knowing that if God wanted this to happen, it would happen. If God didn't want this to happen, for reasons I would never know, I would live with that.

I never plan to turn a problem over to God. The time just comes, as if God is letting me know that I've done my best and it's all right to ask for help. I had asked God for help when I was looking for a business after I had reached a point where I didn't know what to do anymore. It was the same for stopping smoking. My close friend Paul Martin always said to me, "Let go and let God." Sometimes we are just not strong enough to wrestle with the devil by ourselves. We need God in our corner.

I wrote earlier about my compass. I believe this

compass is given to us at birth by God. It's how we know right from wrong. It's a force that guides us throughout our lives to be generous and to help others. It also helps point us in the right direction when we have a difficult problem to solve. I believe as a Christian that if we keep our compass pointing true north by following the Ten Commandments, the light of God's grace will always find us and we will overcome the most difficult challenges we face in life.

Mike showing the "Robin Hood" he shot using a broadhead tip arrow

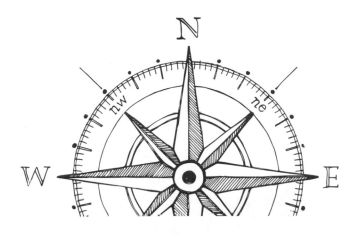

VIII.

Answered Prayers

I stopped hunting in 2003. I started hunting when I was 10 years old and hunted for 41 years. Most of my family and many of my friends were hunters. Hunting was something you were expected to do in the rural area of Southeastern Pennsylvania where I grew up. I loved being outdoors and seeing the indescribable beauty of nature. I relished the physical challenge of hunting. I loved the thrill of the hunt, but I hated the killing. I always cried and prayed after killing an animal. I remember shooting at sparrows with a BB gun when I was a boy. I would cry like a baby if I killed one. When I started to lose my taste for hunting, I made a promise to God that I would stop hunting and killing if I found something that I enjoyed as much that would still keep me connected to nature. I later found that in New Zealand. I believe discovering the wonders of New Zealand was a part of God's plan for me.

I was a serious and skilled archer, and I had the good fortune to go on a number of successful big-game hunts that took me to magnificent parts of the United States and Canada. This included a trip to Cold Bay on the Alaskan Peninsula in 1998 to hunt Alaskan brown bears. That bear is also known as the Kodiak bear, named for Kodiak Island in the Kodiak Archipelago, a group of islands off the southwest coast of Alaska. It is the largest species of the brown bear, and along with the polar bear, it is one of the two largest bears alive today. I had successfully hunted smaller black bears three times with a bow and arrow. I felt comfortable with the danger and confident in my ability, but I had never hunted the larger and more dangerous brown bear.

My hunting trip began with a flight in a small plane from Anchorage, Alaska, to a base camp in the Alaskan wilderness where I joined 11 other hunters. From this base camp, all of us would fly to other camps. The 11 men were rifle hunters. I was the only archer. After we set up camp, the guides asked the other hunters to "shoot their rifles in." The rifle hunters shot at a target to make sure their scopes had not been bumped out of alignment with the gun barrel during travel. After the rifle hunters checked their sight alignment, one of the hunters jokingly said, "The archer hasn't shot in yet." Everyone started laughing. I said to myself, "Oh boy, these guys are throwing down a good-natured challenge," so I went and got my bow and prepared to take some practice shots in front of the other hunters. To add to the challenge, it was raining and extremely windy, which made for very difficult conditions for an archer. A target was placed about 40 yards away from where I was standing. I told everyone that I would never shoot at a bear from that far away, but they told me to practice at that range anyway. A shorter distance improved my chances for the accurate shot placement and the deep penetration that is required to bring down a bear. I had shot animals with a bow and arrow from as far away as 50 yards, but I would not shoot at a bear from 40 yards because of the danger.

The target was made from paper towels that were rolled into the shape of a ball and placed on a sandy hillside about three feet above the base of the hill. I shot a few arrows and placed them in a tight cluster right in the center of the target. One of the rifle hunters knew enough about archery to ask me if I was shooting broadheads or field points. This refers to the design of the tip of the arrow. I was shooting field points. Field points are more accurate than broadheads. Field points are the type of arrow an Olympic archer would use for competition. Broadheads are the type of arrow hunters would use. Broadhead tips are blade-like. The blades make accuracy more difficult because the arrow will "sail." It will move a little left or right or up or down, depending on friction and wind conditions. I was practicing with field points, but I would be hunting with broadheads. The other hunters laughed a little when I told them I was using field points, and they challenged me to shoot at the target with a broadhead. I took an arrow with a broadhead tip out of my bow quiver, placed it on the bow, pulled back, and shot. My broadhead hit one of the arrows in the cluster, split it right down the middle, and stuck in the back of the arrow it had struck. Archers call these shots Robin Hoods. Robin Hoods are very rare: Essentially they are two identical shots, and when they do occur, they are a good indication of the archer's ability. I'm not telling you this to brag; it was actually more luck than it was skill, but it is important that you know I could handle myself with my bow and arrows. My ability as an archer is an important part of the Godly experience I had on this hunt.

Two days before bear season opened, I left the base camp where the 12 of us had gathered and took a 30-minute flight on a private plane along the coast to meet my personal guide. It was a beautiful day to fly. The small plane landed on a beach along the ocean, which was a new experience for me. I had never landed on a beach before. I was happy when the plane landed safely near the site where my guide had set up our base camp and cooking shack. The pilot and I unloaded my gear, and the plane left. We would not be hunting that day because Alaskan hunting laws required that hunters be in camp 24 hours before they start hunting. This prevents spotting and shooting bears from the air, or going to where bears were spotted immediately after hunters have landed.

The second day out was miserable. It was raining hard and was very cold and windy. It was nasty weather, even for Alaska. In the middle of the storm, I noticed a small plane approaching the area where my camp had been set up. I thought the plane might need to land because of the storm and then leave when the storm cleared. The doors opened, and I watched as hunting gear was unloaded and two men got out of the plane. They set up their camp within 200 yards of where my guide and I had set up. This surprised and troubled me. I had planned to be out in the wilderness alone. I had made the long trip to Alaska to hunt by myself.

After I got over my irritation, my guide and I walked over to their camp to introduce ourselves. One of the men was a young preacher, and the other man was the preacher's father. The father was hunting brown bears with a rifle. The preacher was a hunter who lived in the area, but he was not hunting on this trip. He was along to spend time with his father and to serve as his guide. Coincidentally, the preacher's father was from Pennsylvania, where Rhoda and I lived. I was concerned that the father was hunting with a rifle because I would be competing against him with my bow and arrow for the limited number of brown bears we would find. Because we were camped along the ocean, the viable hunting area was reduced. When you set up hunting camp next to water, and not inland, the area that you can reasonably walk to hunt and get back to camp is cut in half because of the water.

The preacher and his father were very friendly. We had a nice visit, shook hands, and wished each other good luck hunting before settling in for the night.

The father shot a bear the day after he arrived. I had seen some bears, but I wasn't able to get close enough to get a good shot. The next day when I left camp with my guide to hunt, we climbed to different spots on a hillside to get a good view of the surrounding area. It was a beautiful sight. I was enjoying looking at the scenery when I heard a rustling sound in the brush. The sound startled me at first, and then I was relieved to see it was the young preacher. He had climbed the hillside to spot bears and to get some exercise. He sat down next to me, and we started to talk about the beauty of the area, what we did for a living, and how he enjoyed living in this part of Alaska. It was an enjoyable talk. From our vantage point on the hillside, we could see a river where the bears fished. We could see this river for miles before it disappeared from our sight. That got us talking about hunting Alaskan brown bears. The preacher reminded me that he lived in the area and that he was very familiar with these animals. He told me several times that he didn't think I should be hunting them with a bow and arrow because they were extremely dangerous. I told him I was an experienced archery hunter and that I didn't feel that I was in danger. I knew of other people who had hunted and shot Alaskan brown bears with a bow and arrow. I wasn't trying to do something that had never been done before.

We talked for three hours before I noticed a brown bear walking along the river heading in our direction. I looked at the preacher and told him, "That's my bear. I'm going to go down to the river and see if I can get close to him." The preacher looked at me and said, "Mike, I'm going to pray for you." I remember that a big smile came over my face and I replied, "Don't worry; I'll see you in church on Sunday." The preacher smiled back, but I could see in his face that he was concerned for my safety.

I headed down the hillside with my guide about 100 yards behind me. I wanted to get within 20 or 30 yards of the bear. The walk to the riverbank to get close to the bear took us about 25 minutes, and all that time I was thinking about what the preacher had said to me about the danger of hunting these animals. "These bears are dangerous... You shouldn't be hunting these bears with a bow and arrow... I'm going to pray for you." I kept hearing those words over and over in my head. I just couldn't free myself of his warning even though I was concentrating on where I was walking and looking for a good spot to position myself to get a shot at the bear. Then, I started praying. "God, please allow me to kill this animal quickly." I was thinking about the animal, not just my own safety. I repeated this prayer with deep sincerity a number of times as

I made my way to the riverbank. "God, please allow me to kill this animal quickly."

The bear was in the river fishing for salmon. I found a relatively open spot on the riverbank where there was some small shrubbery that gave me cover from the bear, but I was not hidden from his sight. I waited patiently as the bear moved through the water toward the spot where I was crouched behind the brush. He was 20 yards away, straight in front of me, when I set myself to take a shot. As he moved further along the river I went to full draw on my bow, taking dead aim at the chest area on the left side of the bear, right behind his shoulder. This is where the bear's heart and lungs are most vulnerable. The instant I was in full draw, the bear swung around to grab a salmon. He missed the salmon, but his momentum turned him back in my direction so we were now facing each other. He looked up and saw me on my knees, aiming right at him. The bear didn't move, and I didn't want to take the shot from a straight-ahead position. A rifle might bring down a bear from a straight-ahead position, but a bow usually will not because the arrow won't penetrate the heavy bones in the front of the bear's chest cavity. In archery hunting, taking this type of shot at a bear at such a close distance would be considered very dangerous because of the high likelihood of wounding the bear and making it angry. Responsible hunters want to kill the animals they hunt quickly, not wound the animal and make it suffer.

I continued to hold my draw on the bear while the bear just stared at me from the river. I had no way of knowing if the bear felt threatened and would approach me or just turn away and leave. Fortunately, the bear turned to leave, and I had the shot at the side of his chest that I wanted. I took aim at the bear from 20 yards. I could easily hit the end of a soda can from that distance, so the shot was well within my range. My draw had weakened a little because of the time I had held my position. I tightened my back to get to a full draw, and I shot. The instant I shot, the bear disappeared into the water, which was between two and three feet deep. I knew that I had hit the bear, but I didn't know where. A bear is not killed that fast with a bow and arrow. I quickly pulled another arrow, expecting the bear to come flying out of the water in a rage, either running at me or running away. Everything had happened so quickly, but the wait for the bear to reappear seemed like forever. All of a sudden, the bear's huge paw came out of the water. I could see that his claws were out, but they were not moving. He was under the water long enough for me to know that he was dead. I thought, "Wow, how did that happen?"

I turned around to locate where my guide was standing. I also looked back up the hill to find the preacher. The preacher had climbed down the hillside to follow me, and he had gotten fairly close to where I was. He was lying on his stomach with his head and shoulders lifted up so he could get a good view of what was occurring. His eyes were as big as saucers. I yelled back to him, "I told you I would see you in church this Sunday."

By now my guide was with me and the preacher. We were standing on the riverbank looking at the huge paw sticking out of the water. We were all amazed at how quickly the bear had dropped. In all my years of hunting, I had never killed an animal so quickly. It would be physically impossible to kill an animal faster. All three of us waded into the river and pulled the bear out of the water and onto the bank. We were all looking for the arrow, but we couldn't see where I had hit the bear because the arrow's shaft had broken off. Then I saw the broken arrow in the back of the bear's head, right where the spine goes into the brain. This was not where I was aiming! I was 20 yards away from the bear and looking at him from the side. I had taken dead aim at the bear's chest right behind the shoulder, but I hit the back of the bear's neck at the base of the skull.

At the back of a bear's skull, there is an opening that exposes the animal's spinal cord as it enters the brain. The arrow had gone right through that opening. The opening is about the width of a broadhead arrow at the widest point of the blades. We could see the marks on the bear's skull where the blades of the arrow passed by the bone. There was just enough room for the arrow to pierce this hole, sever the spinal cord, and instantly kill the bear. It was the best shot I had ever made and the worst shot I had ever made. I missed my target, I wasn't even close, but my prayers were answered to instantly kill the bear. If the errant shot would have had a slightly different line of flight, the outcome could have been very different. Eventually, the bear became a very special part of my trophy room at my farm in Lancaster County, Pennsylvania.

You might think this was a lucky shot. I believe it was a Godly experience. The preacher warned me about the danger, and the preacher's prayers for my safety were answered. My prayers for a quick and painless kill were answered. When I prayed, I was surrendering the outcome of my hunt to God. God answered my prayers by turning a bad shot into the best shot of my life—a one-in-a-million shot. I believe God guided my unsteady hand to protect me and to show mercy to the bear. God heard my prayers and the preacher's prayers. This was not the last time God answered my prayers for help. When you open your heart and mind to God's grace, your prayers will be heard.

Doing what is right often requires sacrifice and sometimes tough love.

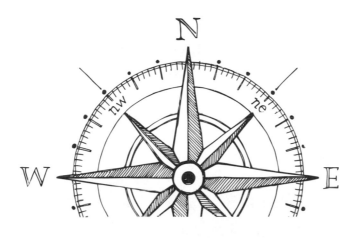

IX.

Love and Loss

I had two Godly experiences in the summer of 2002. One was very frightening, and the other was very enlightening. God guided me through the pain of love and loss so that I had the courage, strength, wisdom, and ability to make two very difficult decisions.

The Passing of My Father

My father, Elton, passed away in June of 2002, after battling emphysema for many years. I had spent a lot of time with him during the last few weeks of his life at a hospital in Tioga County, Pennsylvania, a beautiful and rural part of north central

Pennsylvania. He and his wife, Teena, who cared for and loved my father, lived in a beautiful, rustic, lodge-type home that my dad had built in the area. My father and his friends had hunted in the surrounding woods since the 1940s. I would make the four-hour one-way drive back and forth from Tioga County to my home in Lancaster County to check on my business, get a change of clothes, and pick up anything I could take back to help make my dad as comfortable as possible.

One morning when I was home in Lancaster County, I was taking a shower and praying for my father. I pray in the shower every morning. This is how I start my day. I was praying for my father's comfort during his last days. I was also praying for him because I wondered about his place in Heaven. I had never talked to my father about religion or spiritual matters. I never saw him pray. He might have had strong religious beliefs, but he had never shared them with me. I wanted my father to be accepted into Heaven. During my prayer, I told God that I loved my father and that I would give up my place in Heaven for him. I take what I say to God very seriously, so my offer to give my place in Heaven to my dad was not something I said casually. I prayed, "God, I am very concerned about my father. I'm not sure if you are going to accept him into Heaven, and I am willing to give my place in Heaven to him." At the instant I made this offer to God, a roaring sound, like I had never heard before, came out of my mouth. It was a screaming, agonizing sound. The sound was coming from deep within my chest. It was a sound that a wild animal would make. I had no control over it, and I couldn't stop it. I was buckled over like when you bend down to touch your toes, and I could not breathe. It was terrifying, and I was in great pain. I would estimate the unearthly noise lasted 45 seconds to a minute. When it was over, a dark awareness gripped me. I stood up and said, "I just gave my soul for my father's soul!" I was having difficulty processing what had just occurred, but my first impulse was that my prayer was answered and I had given my place in Heaven to my father. It took me a few minutes to gather myself. I had mixed emotions about this experience. I had made a commitment that I was prepared to live with, but I was also sad about the sacrifice I had made. I got out of the shower, dried off, and got dressed. I didn't say a word to Rhoda, who was sleeping and didn't hear the strange noise I had made. It wasn't until a few years later that I told anyone about this experience.

Two weeks later, my father died. I was with him almost every day during that time. I sat beside his bed when he passed away, and I was one of the last people to see him alive. I was at peace knowing that I had offered my place in Heaven to him. I offered support to Teena, and then returned home to my farm in Lancaster County. Years later, I came to believe that I had not given my place in Heaven to my father. There was a battle in the shower for my soul in exchange for my father's soul. It was a battle of God versus the devil, of good versus evil, of light and darkness, and God won out. I know my father was accepted into Heaven, and I pray there is still a place for me. God clarified for me what had happened. You'll learn more about this when you read about the writing of the Grace Friendship and Partnership Contract in XI Tests of Faith.

Firing My Sons

When I got back to Lancaster County after my father passed away, I ran into Leon, a handyman who worked around our farm. He was building a deer feeder on our property near the farmhouse, and I walked over to say hello to him. He expressed his sympathy for my dad's passing, and then he said, "Oh boy, you missed it!" I asked what he was talking about, and he told me about a terrible fight my sons Elton and Weston had at the farm. Elton was 27 years old and Weston was 25, and both of them worked at Cloister Car Wash in the company's maintenance department. I asked him incredulously, "They were fighting? They were throwing punches?" He confirmed that they were throwing punches and that they had an outright brawl. A few weeks before this, I had called Elton and Weston into the conference room at our corporate office to talk to them about their relationship, both professional and personal. They had been fighting since they were kids, and I'd had enough of it. I was tired of being a referee for their disagreements. I told them, "The next time you fight, I will fire both of you." I told them I wouldn't need to know who had started the next fight, and I wouldn't care what it was about. If they fought again, I would fire both of them, even though this would be tough on me, and a hardship for the company, because they were both valued employees.

I walked back to the farmhouse after talking with Leon to see Rhoda and tell her about my sons' fighting. Rhoda knew about the ultimatum I had given them. She said to me, "You have to do what you think is right." I didn't want to fire my sons. I had just lost my father, and this was the last thing that I needed to deal with. The thought of losing three important men in my life in such a short period of time was overwhelming. I vacillated about what to do. The boys didn't know I knew they had been fighting. I thought maybe I should keep my mouth shut and just let it slide. That would have been the easy way to deal with my conflict.

I went to work the next day and avoided my sons, even though I thought they would want to talk to me about the passing of their grandfather. When I got home that night, I was in turmoil. Should I fire them and live with the pain and loss, including the burden of losing two valuable employees, or back off on my promise to fire them if they fought again? To further complicate my dilemma, I was concerned that firing them would jeopardize our relationship, and their relationship with the rest of our family, forever. I went to bed and fell asleep, but I was suddenly awoken. I walked downstairs and sat on the front porch, just staring into the night. I was overcome with grief, partly for the passing of my father, and partly because I didn't know what to do about my sons. I started to cry uncontrollably. After I stopped, I prayed to God. After I prayed, I cried some more. This emotional roller coaster on the front porch went on for three hours. My eyes were so badly swollen that I looked like I had been in a bare-knuckle fight. After hours of this, I was no closer to knowing what to do than when I first sat on the porch that cool summer night.

It was five o'clock in the morning when I walked back into the house. I noticed two books my Uncle George had recently sent me. When the books had arrived, I thought it was nice of my uncle to send them, but what was I going to do with them? Because I am dyslexic, I don't read books. I had never read a book and rarely even paged through a book other than to glance at photographs. The books were on an end table next to my La-Z-Boy chair. I felt exhausted, so I sat down in the chair and picked up the books just to page through them to look for photos. Both of the books looked very similar. They had photos of deer on the front covers, and I thought they may have something to do with hunting. I quickly went through the first book, but I didn't see anything that caught my eye. Then I picked up the second book, titled *A Look at Life from a Deer Stand,* by Steve Chapman. I was shuffling through the second book, like you would with a deck of cards, when the shuffling stopped at a page about a third of the way into the book. It was early in the morning, and enough light was shining into the room so that I could clearly see the text on the page. There were no photographs to grab my attention, but there was a paragraph that was indented so that it stood out. Despite my difficulty with reading, I was curious enough that I wanted to read the short passage. I went into the kitchen and got my reading glasses, sat back down and turned on the light, and read the following:

> *I have found that I need not fear the struggle my kids go through as they grow and learn. It's the struggle that makes them strong enough to survive. Back on the farm in West Virginia, we hatched baby chicks each spring. I'd see those peepers fighting to peck their way out of the shell and my heart would melt. So to help the tiny things, I decided to peel the shell away for them. To my disappointment, each chick I helped in this way soon died. I didn't know they were developing the strength they needed to survive during the struggle to free themselves from the eggshell. When I denied them the struggle, I robbed them of the stamina they needed to live in the outside world. My kindness killed them.*

Here was my answer to what to do about my sons' fighting. It was a miracle that someone who didn't read found the answer to a problem laid out in black and white on the page of a book. My sons were like the baby chicks. I couldn't protect them. I had to let them go, because that was the only way they would build the strength they needed to live their lives without me protecting them. I raced upstairs to wake up Rhoda. "Read this, read this," I pleaded with her. She woke up quickly because she could tell I was excited about something, and read the words I pointed to on the page. Rhoda looked up at me and said with a hint of relief in her voice, "Well, there's your answer."

I went in to my office the next morning and had termination letters drafted for both Elton and Weston. The termination was effective that day. I called both of them into the conference room, told them I knew about the fight, and told them I was following through on my promise to fire them if they ever fought again. I told them how much I loved both of them. I let them know how difficult this was for me, but I know they didn't understand the pain I was feeling. I'm sure it hurt them, too. I gave them a photocopy of the passage from the book that gave me the insight and the strength to do what I believed was the right thing to do, and I told them how I had miraculously found it in the book. The conversation did not go well, but the changes they eventually made in their relationship with each other convinced me that I had done the right thing. They learned a valuable lesson about getting along. Today, my sons enjoy success in their work, and we share a deep love for each other. Elton and his wife, Megan, live in Pennsylvania and are the proud parents of three boys and four girls. Weston and his daughter enjoy life in Hawaii. I am very proud of them. I believe God was guiding my hand when I picked up that book, opened it, and flipped to page 73. Over the years since, I have given dozens of copies of *A Look at Life from a Deer Stand* to friends and loved ones.

I believe God heard my prayer for my father and then let me know there was a place for him in Heaven. We will experience God's grace when we love deeply enough to be willing to sacrifice ourselves to benefit others. I believe God guided me, a dyslexic man, to find words in a book that would give me the courage, strength, wisdom, and ability to handle a difficult situation with my sons. We will experience God's grace when we pray for guidance to help us in times of trouble. These are two more examples of God's undeserved gifts and love.

In remembrance of Frank, who Mike befriended from 2000—2004

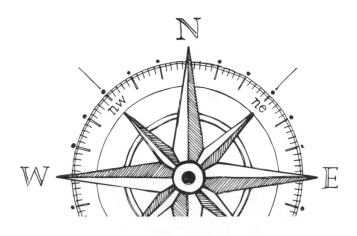

X.

The Homeless

I have always felt drawn to the homeless. I think the homeless are God's chosen people because they challenge us to show our humanity, the depth of our love, and our courage. I have always believed I experienced God's presence when I was with the homeless.

My wife, Rhoda, believes that I find homeless people, but I think we find each other. They don't come up to me and ask for something, and I don't openly look for them. It's a mutual awareness, as if our paths were made to cross for no apparent reason.

My encounters with the homeless were infrequent at first, but then they started to occur more often. The encounter has always been with a male, never a female, and their ages have ranged from 40 to 60 years old. It's hard to tell the age of a homeless man because he is usually dirty, unshaven, and dressed in ways that hide his age.

I always try to be friendly and generous with the homeless people I meet, usually in small ways like buying sandwiches or sharing fruit and candy. I try to engage them in conversation. Most of my experiences have been no more involved than that. The closeness I feel for them is deep. I feel good about offering a helping hand and seeing the appreciation that is returned. I hope every encounter I have had made us both feel better. Two of my experiences with the homeless were life-changing. They were gifts of love from God.

Frank

My first noteworthy experience with a homeless person occurred in 2000, when I was building my third car wash in Lancaster, Pennsylvania. Right next to the wash was a lumberyard with a six-foot-high wooden fence that separated the two properties. I could see over this fence because my side was elevated. In the lumberyard, there were a number of abandoned cars that were backed up against the fence.

One evening, I noticed a homeless man getting

into one of the cars to sleep. It was cold, late fall or winter, and there was snow on the ground. The following night, I saw him get into the car again. I walked around the fence and tried to approach him, but the moment he saw me coming, he jumped out and ran away. I watched him come and go for days, but I was wary of approaching again, so I kept my distance. One morning, after I saw him leave, I folded a $20 bill and put it in the air-conditioning vent at the front of the car. The next day I checked to see if he had taken the money, but it was still there. My curiosity was aroused, so I replaced the $20 with a $50, and finally a $100 bill. He never touched the money.

Eventually, the man did allow me to approach him as long as I kept a distance. As far as I could tell, I was the only one who tried to help him and talk to him, even though he never said a word. One day I told him I was going to leave the car wash open at night so he could stay inside and keep warm. I told him to use the restroom where there was a sink to wash his face and hands. My managers were very uncomfortable with this, warning me that he was going to steal or ruin something. My response shocked them. "If he steals something, we'll replace it. If he ruins something, we'll fix it. I want the building left open!"

I couldn't tell whether he was going into the building at night or not. When I saw him again, I asked if he came inside. To my surprise, he spoke. "No, it has the devil in there," he said. When I questioned what he meant, he said, "Red and black," referring to our corporate colors and the colors we were painting the inside of the building. I tried to reassure him that the devil wasn't there and that he should come inside at night, but I couldn't convince him. Most homeless people are homeless for a reason. Clearly he did not think rationally, but I didn't know that until we had our first brief conversation.

Throughout the winter, I continued to try to help him. One evening after dark when I went to check on him, Rhoda was with me. He got out of the car he was in and started walking toward us, stopping 20 feet away as he always did. He was now talking to me, and occasionally I could get close to him. I found out that his name was Frank, and I felt we had built some trust between us. When I got out of the truck to greet him, I noticed his eyes glaring at Rhoda, who had remained in the truck. When he realized someone was with me, he turned around and took off into the night.

Two years had passed since the first night I

approached him. It would have been easy to give up on Frank, but I felt compelled to try to help him. One weekend I was at a sporting show in Harrisburg, Pennsylvania when I came across a booth where a man was making IDs that reminded me of Army dog tags. I asked him to make a tag that said "My name is Frank" on one side and "In case of emergency call Mike Mountz" and my phone number on the other side. I carried the tag in my pocket for months before I saw Frank again, riding his bike near my home in Ephrata. I drove past him on the opposite side of the road, then turned around and passed him again. I parked and waited for him to approach me. When he saw it was me, he stopped. I asked him how he was doing, and he said something I'll never forget: "I read an article about you." I was dumbfounded. I didn't know he could read. He had been rummaging through a Dumpster and had come across a newspaper article about me and the new car wash I had built in Lancaster. I talked with him for a few minutes, then I handed him some fruit and candy and told him about the tag I had made and asked him to put it on. He shook his head and refused to take it. I tried to convince him, but he wouldn't take it, and I knew not to push. I put the tag back in my pocket with the hope he would change his mind when I saw him again.

I told Frank we were only a few miles from my home, and I asked him if he knew where I lived. To my surprise, he said he did. I had no idea how he knew this, and I didn't probe for any details. I told him the ground-level basement door was always open, and there was a bed next to the door where he could sleep. He told me when I saw him again that he did ride his bike to my house one day to check it out, but he didn't come inside. I was discouraged that Frank wouldn't accept more of my help, but I was determined to keep trying.

The next time I saw Frank, it was a snowy Christmas day. Rhoda and I had moved to our farm since the last time I saw Frank. This was the fourth winter after I had met him huddled in the car parked against the fence in Lancaster. When I would see him in Lancaster, it was easy to keep tabs on him, but the car he slept in was long gone, and by now I was losing touch with Frank. Late that night, Rhoda and I were making our way home through six inches of fresh snow after visiting with her family and then checking on our car wash in Ephrata. This was not a night to be out. It was well below freezing and very windy. The roads had not been plowed, so I was driving very carefully in my 4-wheel drive pick-up truck, trying to stay in the tire tracks that had already been made by another vehicle. Because I was keeping such a close eye on the road, I noticed very thin tire tracks leading to the parking lot of a grocery store we were about to pass. I turned around and drove back to the tire tracks. I thought the smaller tracks were probably bicycle tracks, and I said to Rhoda, "I bet that's Frank!" We drove into the parking lot, following the bike tracks to a shed that was used by Amish customers to hitch their horse-drawn carriages. The shed had a hay loft, about four feet off the ground, designed so the horses could pull hay through the slats of the loft. I swung my truck around so the headlights were shining directly into the shed, and the first thing I saw was a bicycle parked against the wall.

I didn't see Frank at first, but when I looked more closely, I saw him sleeping in the hay loft. The only way to describe the scene was that it looked like someone lying in a manger. I couldn't believe my eyes. I knew if I woke Frank and asked him to come home with us, he wouldn't do it. Frank had rejected my offers of help too many times for me to think differently.

Rhoda and I decided to leave, and all the way home I was tormented about what to do. When I got home, I was very upset and decided to gather the best winter hunting clothing I had to take to Frank. I told Rhoda my plans, and she asked me to wait while she made a thermos of chicken noodle soup. I grabbed the clothing and the thermos and made the 10-mile trip back to the shed where Frank was sleeping. When I got there, I parked about 50 feet away, focused my headlights on the hay loft, and walked through six inches of snow to within five feet of him. I stood there like a child, staring at him sleeping in his bed of hay, and I just started crying. I looked at him for five minutes. He looked so peaceful, and I felt so helpless. I thought, "How can this be?" I wanted to help him, but there was nothing I could do. I asked myself whether I would want to be startled awake from a peaceful sleep at one o'clock in the morning, and I decided not to wake him. I knew that Frank would not accept any offer of help, so what point would there be to waking him up? I placed the clothing and thermos of soup next to his bike and left.

Later, on my way to work one morning, I passed a homeless man riding a bike in the opposite direction that I was driving. I slowed down to get a good look at him to see if it was Frank. It looked like him, but I wasn't sure. It was always hard to tell with a quick glance because his appearance was so unkempt and the things he carried on his bike were constantly changing. I turned around, drove past him, and parked my truck on the opposite side of the street and watched him ride toward me. When he got close, I yelled, "Hey, Frank!" The man quickly turned his bike, crossed the street, and pulled up right next to me. I found this a little curious. When Frank would get close to me, he always approached timidly, not with the ease with which you would greet a close friend you hadn't seen for a while. I asked, "How have you been, Frank?" "Okay," he replied with a friendly smile. We talked, and he was far more talkative than usual. I still wasn't sure this was Frank. Then it dawned on me how to find out. I reached in my pocket for money and peeled off two $20 bills. I handed the money to him, and he quickly took it. I knew instantly that this was not Frank. In all the years I had tried to help Frank, he never took my money. I couldn't force money on him. I didn't let on I knew he wasn't Frank. I told the man to have a good day and to take care of himself, and off he went. He was homeless, and I was happy to help him.

I got back into my truck to head to work when all of a sudden a powerful feeling came over me. The feeling was so strong that I sensed an outside presence taking hold of my thoughts and emotions. For me, it was a Godly experience. I said out loud,

"If that ever happens again, God, shame on me!" I had $150 in my pocket, and I gave him $40. Why didn't I give him all the money in my pocket? I was heading back to my office, and all I had to do was ask the office manager to go into the safe and replace the cash. It would have been that easy. Why did I give only part of myself? Why didn't I give all of myself? In that instant, I made a promise to God that if ever again I was with someone in need and I had cash in my pocket, I would give it all. My promise to give it all was soon going to be tested.

I continued to look for Frank when I traveled in Lancaster County. I wanted to help him in any way that I could. As it turned out, the Christmas night at the shed was the last time I saw him.

I saw this prayer in a church bulletin, and it reminded me of Frank:

> *Christ is the good shepherd*
> *who knows and cares for every one of*
> *the sheep in different folds.*
> *In Christ there is neither Jew nor Gentile;*
> *in Christ there is no discrimination of*
> *gender, class or race.*
> *In Christ the poor are blessed, the simple*
> *receive truth hidden from the wise.*

A Test of My Promise

My company was in the process of opening our fourth location in Reading, Pennsylvania. This facility was the largest of its kind in the world, and the project had consumed my time and energy for a year. Rhoda knew that we needed a little break, so she made plans one evening for us to go out. She never put pressure on me to be on time, but I knew it was important to her for me to be on time that night. I left Reading a little later than I should have to drive 30 miles back to my Lancaster County home. As I passed a convenience store 10 miles from my Ephrata car wash, I noticed a man sitting at a picnic table at the side of the property. Because of his appearance, I thought he was homeless. "That's a homeless person, that's a homeless person," I said to myself as the urge to help him gripped me. I was filled with conflict because I knew if I stopped, I was going to be later than I already was to meet Rhoda.

I didn't think about it for long. I hit the brakes, turned around, and pulled into the parking lot. I went into the store and bought two bottles of water, then walked over to the picnic table and sat down behind the man. He was wearing a dirty lightweight coat, and his long blond hair covered the side of his face and hung down to his shoulders. He also had an Army-type duffle bag with him. We sat in silence for a few minutes before I offered him a bottle of water and asked how he was doing. He told me that he saw electricity coming out of the pole in front of us, and he was watching the electricity move down the pole and go into the ground. "Do you see that?" he asked very casually. I told him I didn't, but I was sure he did. I kept talking, but he had very little to say. I did find out he was on his way to Lancaster, which was 30 miles away. I assumed he was walking or hitchhiking because there was no bike, and I still had not seen his face because he had not turned to speak to me.

I offered to drive him to Ephrata, where I was going to meet Rhoda. He would still have a 20-mile trip to Lancaster. He accepted my offer, grabbed his duffle bag, and got into my truck with me. He sat on the front seat with his back toward me and his duffle bag between his legs, looking out the side window. After we had driven a short distance, I asked him a question. I'm not sure why, but I just blurted it out without any prompting. "I'm just curious," I said. "Do you believe in God?" He turned and looked at me for the first time. His gaze went through me like the electricity he said he saw when we were sitting on the bench. I felt like he was looking into my soul.

The sensation was so strong that I believed he was God, or he was sent by God, and I was staring directly into his eyes. At that moment there was no doubt in my mind he was divine. I had never seen eyes like his before—a deep, piercing blue that literally took my breath away. As I stared into his eyes, I felt I could see his soul. His eyes were set off by the most beautiful, friendly smile I had ever seen. He looked like a man in his fifties, and he struck me as someone who was very wise.

I was stunned, like I was having an out-of-body experience, but I wasn't scared. A few moments passed before he answered my question about his belief in God. "Yes, I do!" he said with such conviction, with such believability, that it shocked me. I didn't know what to say or do. I was totally caught off guard. I felt as though God had just spoken to me. A few more minutes passed, and he asked me, "Do you want to know what day God started flooding the earth?" I said, "Yes, that would be wonderful," thinking to myself, *This can't be happening* and *How would he know that?* He then opened his duffle bag and pulled out a beautiful brown leather binder. I recall wondering where he got such a well-crafted and expensive-looking binder. He opened the binder and slowly paged through it. There were graphs, charts, and numbers on every page, but no written text or photographs. The pages were off-white, but very clean. Each page was different, and the graphs and charts were beautifully done, not scribbled. I was looking at the book and trying to keep my eyes on the road. He thumbed through the binder, and when he got to the middle pages, he said, "2,192,047 days ago." I was comfortable enough for a smile to cross my face, and I asked him, "Are you sure about that?" "Yes, I'm sure," he responded, looking deep into my eyes with a friendly, knowing, matter-of-fact confidence. When I asked him if that was the day the earth was flooded, he corrected me and said that it was the day the rain began. I asked ministers, nuns, and knowledgeable friends if they could verify this information, and they couldn't say if it was accurate or not. I didn't feel a need to question it, because I felt I was in the presence of God or a messenger of God. I know he believed it was accurate, and that was good enough for me.

We drove another 10 miles and reached the spot where I needed to drop him off so I could make my way home to Rhoda. My feelings for this man were so intense by now that there was no way I could just let him out of the truck and leave. I was in a rare spiritual place that's hard to describe. I knew I was late to meet Rhoda, and getting myself deeper in trouble by the minute, but I had to offer him something more than just a short ride. I decided to take him to a motel that was nearby. It was one of those country motels with 25 rooms and two cars in the parking lot. It was rarely full. I pulled in, saw the VACANCY sign, and told him I would get him a room and come back tomorrow to take him to Lancaster. As we walked up to the office, the sign suddenly changed to NO VACANCY. A woman came out and said, "No rooms. No vacancy!" I told her I had just seen the vacancy sign, and I could see there were only a handful of cars in the parking lot. She said again, this time much louder and very harshly, "No rooms! There's no vacancy!" I started to argue with her, but the homeless man grabbed my arm and calmly said, "It's okay," and pulled at me to leave. It wasn't okay, but I didn't want to make the situation worse than it already was, so we got back in my truck and left.

I knew Rhoda was probably getting annoyed waiting for me, but I decided I was going to drive this man to Lancaster and face the music at home later. As we were driving away, I remembered that there was another motel just down the road, much like the place that had just turned us away. When we arrived, I noticed a VACANCY sign again, so we parked under the carport and walked into the lobby. I told the man working the desk I wanted to get a room for my friend. "I won't rent one to him!" he said. My anger started to build again as I pointed out that the sign said they had a vacancy. "I won't rent one to you!" he repeated defiantly. I explained I was the owner of Cloister Car Wash, which was right down the road in the neighboring town. I offered my business card and credit card and explained that I would pay for the room and cover any other costs he might be concerned about. He reluctantly agreed and rented me a room for the night.

We got the key to the room, and my homeless friend settled in. I was really anxious about getting home to Rhoda, but I needed to know something. I asked him to write down the number of days he told me had passed since God started flooding the earth. I gave him a piece of paper and a pen, and he wrote down the same number he had given me when we were driving in my truck: 2,192,047 days. He also wrote, "Noah, day of the Lord, in Genesis, the day it started raining." This happened on August 12, 2005, the day I felt I met either God dressed as a homeless man, or a messenger of God.

It was time for me to leave. I reached into my pocket to give him money and felt a large amount of cash that was left over from a business trip Rhoda and I had just taken. It was almost $1,000 that I had intended to return to the office, but I had forgotten to do it. I started to peel off a few bills, and then I remembered the promise I had made to God: "I will give my all." My "all" at that moment was a lot of money, but a promise to God is a promise I had to honor. So I folded the stack of cash, took the man's hand, put the cash in his palm, and gently closed his hand over the money. We exchanged hugs, said goodbye, and out the door I went.

It's worth noting that the man I befriended did not make an especially bad appearance. You could tell he was homeless, but he wasn't filthy dirty or acting unusually. If I ran a motel, I would have rented a room to him. I didn't understand why the two motels gave us such a hard time, but I never felt animosity toward them. Years later, as I reflected on this experience, I came to believe that it was a test to see whether I would give up or fight for this man. It was part of a perfect plan God had for me.

I have no regrets about living up to my promise to give my all. I do wish I would have gone back a few hours later, or early the next morning, to see if the man was still there. I was out with Rhoda, and it got to be late, so I just didn't check. I talked with the motel manager later the next day and found out there was no damage to the room and that nothing had been taken, but I didn't ask if he had slept in the bed. I often wonder if he stayed, or just waited for me to drive away before he disappeared into the night. I even wonder if he was real or a Heavenly presence that came to earth and into my life to see whether I would live up to my promise.

One thousand dollars is a lot to give to anyone, let alone a stranger. I thought about that as I was taking the money from my pocket, but I gave it to him with peace of mind and joy in my heart. I believe that meeting this homeless man was not only a test of my promise to God, but also an affirmation of the opportunities that we are all given to know God's grace. Sometimes we don't see them, or we react to them like the motel managers, and the opportunity is lost. When we do respond, we can know God's undeserved gifts and love.

I never did get the man's name. It's strange that I didn't ask, but I didn't. I was so astounded by the power of his presence and the events that occurred in our brief encounter that his name didn't seem to matter to me. What mattered was that I was kind, showed courage to help, and kept my promise to give my all. My sense of God's presence was sharpened, and I was ready to see if I was worthy of more opportunities to experience God's grace.

Faith is the light of the world that will help you find your way.

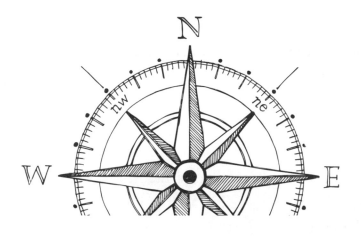

XI.

Tests of Faith

Author's Disclosure: For this experience, some names have been changed for privacy reasons.

"There's Something Special about Him"

In the fall of 2004, I received a phone call from Jeff, a businessman whom I did not know. He asked me if he and his brother-in-law, Roger, could visit our car wash in Lancaster and if I would be willing to give them a tour of the facility. Both men were from Canada. Over the years, people from all over the world visited our four car washes. The visitors were mostly car wash operators or entrepreneurs who were interested in getting into the business. Cloister enjoyed a reputation as a unique and successful operation. We were a high-volume and a higher-price wash, which was unusual. We also introduced many innovations that other operators wanted to see and learn more about. I was always happy to show people through our facilities, and I always tried to make myself available when they visited. I believe strongly in the philosophy "live, learn, and pass it on."

We agreed that we would meet on Saturday, but they didn't show up. Jeff called that night to apologize, and we rescheduled for after church on Sunday. My general manager, Jim, and I greeted our guests when they arrived midafternoon. We were joined by two other managers. It had gotten later than I expected, and I told Roger and Jeff that I was tight on time because I had to get to Reading, Pennsylvania, about 45 minutes away. I had to make a decision that day if I was going to buy land to build a fourth car wash. The Reading project would be huge in scope compared to industry standards and larger than our facilities in Lancaster, York, and Ephrata. It would be 44,000 square feet under roof, on seven acres of property, employing 100 people. I wanted to walk the property one more time before I made my decision. I offered to start the tour by walking them through the lube shop, the quick oil change part of our business. I also wanted to explain to them how we used the oil we drained from the cars to heat the buildings in the winter and to heat the water we used to wash cars year-round. They weren't interested in hearing about or seeing the lube shop. I thought to myself, why would they travel all the way from Canada and not want to look at an important part of the operation?

We all walked to the wash tunnel building and into the equipment room. Roger asked me a question while we were in the equipment room that gave me pause. I had given many tours of our facilities, and the questions I was asked tended to be typical everyday operational and equipment questions: How many cars did we wash? What equipment and chemicals did we use? What was our labor rate? His question was a very insightful and probing question that touched on the essence of what made our company different and successful. It was a much deeper question than I would typically get. I didn't know a lot about the two men, but I did know they didn't own car washes, so the clarity of his question surprised me. We moved to another part of the facility, and Roger asked me another question, similar in depth to the one he asked a few minutes earlier. Now I started to think, *Who is this guy*?

After Roger asked a third impressive and very serious question, I knew there was something special about him, and I was eager to learn more about him. When the tour was over, we gathered in the conference room, where I offered to answer any other questions. I was in a hurry to get to Reading, but my curiosity about my visitors had been tweaked. Roger asked a fourth profound question that I recall was about how we manage the uncertainty of the weather, and now I thought to myself, *You're in a chess match with this guy. He knows exactly what he's talking about. He's testing me to see if I know what I'm talking about.*

I had to get to Reading, and I suggested to Roger and Jeff that they visit with my managers for as long as they wanted. I gave Roger a copy of our employee handbook. Roger offered to send me a case of wine to thank me and my managers for our time. I declined the wine and pointed out in the employee handbook our policy of not accepting gifts or gratuities. I told Roger this applied to everyone, including me.

As I was driving to Reading, I wanted to think about the decision I had to make on the property, but I could not get Roger out of my mind. I got to Reading with about a half hour of daylight left to walk the property when I got a phone call from

Bill Barclay, a good friend and a successful car wash operator from Springfield, Missouri. I didn't have the time to get involved with a lengthy phone call, but I decided to take the call anyway. We talked until it was dark. I never did walk the property that night, but I did agree a few days later to buy the land and move ahead with construction planning. Bill's call was an example of God's grace because it led to something that spiritually changed my life. You'll read about this in Chapter XII, Carmelite Nuns.

After I hung up from my call, I got in my truck to head home and called Jim to see how the visit in Lancaster had turned out. I asked Jim if our guests had stayed after I left. "No," he replied with a hint of surprise in his voice. "Your taillights weren't out of the parking lot and they were leaving." I questioned him, "You're telling me that they came all the way from Canada to visit for only two hours, and they didn't hang around, ask questions, or take any literature or other information?" Jim said all that they took was the employee handbook I had given Roger. I asked if they took any photographs, and Jim told me they took one photo of the property as they were leaving. I was perplexed and more curious than I was earlier about our visitors. I told Jim, "There's something very special about Roger. I don't know if he's very smart or very rich. I don't know what it is, but there's just something special about him."

There was nothing showy or egotistical about Roger. He was not wearing an expensive watch. He was dressed like any person you might pass on the street. He was driving a very common rental car, and he didn't speak like a man who held himself above others. Despite this, I had a very strong gut feeling that Roger was a very accomplished man, and that we were about to be connected in some way. More than anything else, the questions he had asked me made me feel this way. Little did I know that meeting Roger would set in motion what would become my most significant Godly experience.

A few days later, I received a letter from Roger. He thanked me and my team for showing him and Jeff around our Lancaster facility, and he said that he had looked through our employee handbook and that he noticed Cloister had donated money to numerous causes. He shared with me that he donated money to organizations that were important to him. This included a recent $500,000 donation to his personal charity, a foundation that he created. For a second or two, I thought that this was a typo and that he must have added one or two many zeros. I quickly realized he meant $500,000. I called Jim and said to him, "I don't know how smart

Roger is, but he certainly is rich!" We laughed about this, and I showed the letter to other people in our office.

Shortly after I received Roger's letter, he and Jeff visited again. On this trip we toured our facilities in Lancaster, York, and Ephrata.

A week or two after his second visit, I received a phone call from Roger to ask me if he could meet with me again. He accepted my offer to stay with Rhoda and me at our farm 10 miles from the Ephrata car wash. When he arrived, we got him settled in, and we visited for a while with our friend Ned Pelger, whom we had invited to stop by to meet Roger. I had told Ned about Roger's $500,000 donation and the insightful questions he had asked me, and Ned was eager to meet him. We all had an enjoyable conversation, and Ned and Roger exchanged contact information before Ned had to leave. During his visit at the farm, Roger told me that he was interested in building car washes and wanted to talk more about a partnership with me. This intrigued me. A partnership with Roger might make sense in the future, but we did not discuss any details that night. I told Roger I would like to think about his proposal and that I would get back to him. He left for Canada the next morning.

I did some research on Roger and found out that

he was a very successful and wealthy man. I wanted to know more about what he was thinking. Soon after Roger's visit to the farm, we had the chance to talk some more when he joined me on a trip to Germany to visit with my friend Joe Enning. Joe operated many large and successful car washes in Germany, and was highly regarded as a top-notch businessman and one of the best car wash operators in the world.

A few weeks after our Germany trip, Roger called me and asked if I could meet him at the Harrisburg airport. He told me not to go to the main terminal, but to a terminal next to the main building. He told me I would see a guard at the entrance to this building and that I should tell him that I was there to meet him. The guard escorted me into the facility, which was also a large hangar. I was taken into a huge conference room with a conference table that must have seated 30 to 40 people. I was the only one in the room, and I was thinking to myself, *What the heck is going on here?*

After I waited about five minutes, Roger walked in. We chatted for a few minutes, but I could see that he was eager to get down to business. "Here," he said, "I want to show you something and get your opinion." He grabbed a blueprint and rolled it out on the conference table in front of me. It was a blueprint for a car wash. When it comes to designing car washes, my ideas can get "far out there" with the design of equipment and facilities. I'm proud to say this has led to many innovations that can be found at Cloister locations and at other car washes in the United States and around the world. In 2000, the International Car Wash Association gave Cloister their Leadership in Innovation Award. What Roger was showing me was way beyond anything that I had ever thought about. He had designed a car wash that used a circular design to do interior cleaning. If you wanted the interior cleaned, you would pull your car into a slot. Then your car would rotate around in a circle, from station to station, where each cleaning task would be completed. When it reached the final slot, it was backed out, ready to drive away. The concept was similar to the mechanism that rotates a revolving restaurant. The reason for this revolutionary concept was because the cost of land in larger cities was very high, and this idea dramatically reduced the amount of land that would be required to build a car wash. This idea was so far out there that I just kept staring at the drawings to get my head around the concept. Many minutes went by as I just kept looking at the blueprints. I didn't even look up at Roger, who was pacing back and forth behind me.

What happened next was spontaneous. I calmly and very seriously said, "Roger, do you believe in God?" The question was not planned. It was not part of an evaluation process I went through. It just came out of my mouth as if God was reminding me there was a lot at stake here and I couldn't forget to ask this. He immediately said, "No, I don't. I don't believe in God." He quickly added that his very best friend, Tom, was a very spiritual person and that Tom "totally believes in God." He told me that Tom would vouch for his character and that he would tell me Roger was a good person.

We didn't talk much more about Roger's disbelief in God. I told Roger this was a lot to think about and that I couldn't give him an answer right then. This meeting took place on Saturday, and I committed to Roger to let him know if I was interested in further discussion about a partnership by the following Friday. This partnership would be to build Roger's circular design car washes in Canada, and eventually throughout the world. I had a lot to think about.

Guided by the Hand of God

I drove back to my farm in Lancaster County. I wanted to talk to Rhoda, but she was not home, so

I got on my tractor and started mowing the property. This was the best thing I could do to collect my thoughts about what had just occurred with Roger. When I saw Rhoda, I told her about my meeting with Roger, and she asked me if I had any idea what to do. "I have no clue. I just don't know," I told her with a mix of confusion, exhilaration, and exasperation. All day Sunday and Monday, I thought about and prayed about Roger's proposal. I was very frustrated that I couldn't even find a starting point to work my way through how to handle this challenge and opportunity.

On Tuesday, I still didn't have any idea about what I wanted to do. I went to bed late, but woke up at 2 am. I wake up a number of times at night, but this "awakening" was different. I had the feeling that I was being pulled or summoned somewhere. This was something I had never experienced before. I sat on the side of the bed with my feet on the floor and thought to myself, *What is going on here?* I didn't hear a voice speaking to me, but I had the sensation that I was being guided by an outside force. The first message was, "Get up and put on your robe." This was unusual because I never put my robe on when I got up during the night. The next message was, "Slip on your shoes." After I put on my robe and slipped on a pair of loafers, I was instructed to "go downstairs." As I was walking down the wooden steps of the farmhouse, I thought that I would turn right at the bottom of the steps and walk into the living room or kitchen. About three-quarters of the way down the steps, I realized that I was being drawn outside. I was completely aware of what was happening to me, but I didn't understand why it was happening. I didn't try to resist, because I wanted to know what this was all about. I opened the door, took a few steps outside, and then was transformed into a childlike state. I was in this state for 45 to 60 seconds. I felt totally free, without fears or concerns, like a child would feel when they are with their father. I started to walk, knowing that I was holding God's hand, without a care or worry in the world. I walked about 30 yards from the back door of the farmhouse, up a series of steps, and almost to the porch at the back of the barn. I wasn't questioning or thinking about what was occurring. As I approached the porch, the feeling of being in a childlike state faded away, and I went back to being myself. I felt a deep, blissful, indescribable peace. I remember smiling and thinking, *Wow, what a beautiful experience that was!*

I walked into my trophy room at the back of the barn, which I also used as an office. Within seconds of entering the trophy room, I got another message. This message guided me to sit at the back of the bar looking into the area where my hunting trophies were on display. It was now a little after 2 am. I was questioning what was going on, and I asked myself, *Why am I sitting here and looking into the trophy room?* The instant I said that, my hand reached for some loose paper that was on top of the bar, and I started writing. I struggled with writing, just as I did with reading, because of my dyslexia. I wasn't struggling now. I was writing and creating drawings and graphs rapidly. I would finish a page, toss it aside, and create another drawing on a new page. It felt like only a few minutes had passed, and I had created 11 pages of information that I didn't understand, but that I knew was complete. I didn't feel a need to change anything. There was no doubt in my mind that what had just been created was perfect, and there was nothing for me to add or change. This was extremely unusual for me. My nature is always to design or build something and then change it to make it better. Anyone who has worked with me knows that I change everything I do a few times before I feel I have what I want. What I created at the bar was different. It was done. There was nothing more to think about. Then it occurred to me what had just happened. God had guided my hand to write a contract between God, Roger, and me. I wrote the contract for God. I cried uncontrollably for a few minutes before I regained my composure. The solution for what to do about Roger's proposal was scattered in front of me. Once again, God had helped me find a solution to a problem. It was another Godly experience, and the ultimate example of God's grace.

I gathered all the papers and stared at them with wonderment. There were graphs and charts with names, titles, and supporting text. When I look at this material now, I would estimate it would take me days to create what I did that night in minutes. The contract included peoples' names. Randy Fox, a deacon at his Mennonite church and the head of maintenance at Cloister, was one of the names. He had worked at Cloister for only a few months. Why was his name included? My friend Ned Pelger, an engineer, and my Methodist minister Dennis Snovel were included along with Roger, Roger's close and very spiritual friend Tom, and me. At this moment I didn't understand why these people were part of the contract. Later, I came to understand that God knew the support of these people was critically important if my partnership with Roger was going to be successful.

Witness to God's Love and Grace

I left the documents on the bar in my trophy room, and I walked outside to sit on the porch of the barn. It was now around 3 am. I sat there as my mind went through what had occurred over the past hour. God woke me up, had me get dressed, put me in a child-like state, and led me to a place where God guided my hand to create a Grace Friendship and Partnership Contract between God, Roger, and me. I broke down and started crying again. This lasted for a while, 15 to 20 minutes, before I regained my composure. I felt totally drained emotionally. As I reflected on how amazing this was, I looked up a hill that was just beyond the back porch where I was sitting. The crest of this hill was the highest part of the property, and it was a beautiful place from which to look down on the farm. There was a large rock on the hill for me to sit on that was placed there by a bulldozer during work on the farm, but I was always working and never found the time to do that. I had asked men who were working on the property to move the rock to another spot nearby that offered a better view of the surroundings. As I was sitting there, I started to feel drawn to go see if the rock had been moved to the exact spot that I wanted, so I got up to walk up the hill to take a look.

There was a decent amount of moonlight, so I could see where I was going. I hadn't walked more than a few steps when I was put back into the same child-like state that I was in earlier. This also lasted for 45 to 60 seconds and then faded away. Once again, I felt like I was in the presence of God as I walked toward the rock at the top of the hill. When I was within a few feet of the rock, I felt myself leaving the childlike state again. I wanted to walk to the front of the rock, but I was drawn by a force to the rear of the rock. As I stood behind the rock, I was literally driven to my knees—pushed down with force to a kneeling position. This was the second time in my life that this had happened to me. I wrote about the first time in Chapter IV Driven to My Knees. As I knelt down, I recited three prayers. I was familiar with two of them, The Lord's Prayer and the 23rd Psalm, but I would not have been able to repeat three words of those prayers before that night if I had to. Now I was passionately reciting these prayers out loud from beginning to end. I soon adopted the third prayer as a road map for how to live my life.

The Lord's Prayer: Our Father who art in Heaven, hallowed be thy name. Thy Kingdom come. Thy will be done on earth as it is in Heaven. Give us this day our daily bread, and forgive us our debts, as we forgive our debtors. And lead us not into temptation, but deliver us from evil. For thine is the kingdom, and the power, and the glory, forever and ever. Amen.

Psalm 23: The Lord is my shepherd; I shall not want. He maketh me to lie down in green pastures: he leadeth me beside the still waters. He restoreth my soul: he leadeth me in the paths of righteousness for his name's sake. Yea, though I walk through the valley of the shadow of death, I will fear no evil: for thou art with me; thy rod and thy staff they comfort me. Thou preparest a table before me in the presence of mine enemies: thou anointest my head with oil; my cup runneth over. Surely goodness and mercy shall follow me all the days of my life: and I will dwell in the house of the Lord forever.

Mike's Prayer: God, give me the courage, the strength, the wisdom, and the ability to be a good Christian, to be a good husband, to be

a good father, and to be a good employer. In
God's name I pray. Amen.

I was so emotional that it was difficult to stay in the kneeling position. I felt like I was going to collapse. I mustered the strength to stand up and walked around to the front of the rock and sat down. Every ounce of energy had been drawn out of me, but the feeling was blissful, like I had totally surrendered to God. I said to God, "You have given me so many wonderful moments with you, not just tonight, but throughout my life. I don't need any more. I have been blessed. I've had more than my fair share of your love. Please share your grace with others." The moment after I said this, it was revealed to me that I had not given my soul for my father's place in Heaven when I prayed for him in the shower before he passed away. This revelation was so overwhelming to me that I felt I was totally in God's hands. There had been an intense battle between good and evil for my soul. The force of God prevailed. The unforgettable roaring sound that was coming out of me was because the battle for my soul had hurt so badly. The revelation was not a voice that I heard out loud, but a voice I heard inside me—inside my soul. It was a feeling more than a sound. I didn't hear it in my ear; I felt it inside of me. It was the same thing that I experienced earlier when I was told to put on my robe and shoes and when I was guided to write the Grace contract documents in the trophy room.

God wasn't done with me yet, however. God gave me another miracle. This was an insight, a vision in my mind that I refer to as "on earth as in Heaven." I still have difficulty interpreting what I saw, but at the time I believed it was a glimpse of what our world would be like if we all accepted God into our lives. Today, I believe I was shown a glimpse of Heaven. I had a picture in my mind of something that was peaceful and very beautiful. It came to me with a clarity that can't be described in words. I was seeing and feeling peace and beauty like I had never experienced before in my life. This vision stayed in my mind for 5 to 10 seconds and then it was gone. I can't describe it today. God had let me see a glimpse of Heaven and then purposefully took it away from me. I believe that this was God's way of strengthening my faith.

I was crying uncontrollably again. I was more exhausted and drained than I had been earlier in the evening or at any other time in my life. It took me at least 10 minutes to regain my composure. I was sitting on the rock at the spot where I had asked the workers to move it, looking over my property and reflecting on what had just occurred, when I thought that this was still not the best spot for the rock. Typical of me, I had to change the location again. As before, I was drawn to walk to another spot about 100 yards higher up the hill, which I now thought would give me the most optimal view of the property. I paced back and forth to check different views of the farm. The precise spot was important to me because in addition to the view, I wanted this to be the place where I would sit with nature and pray.

As I stood there thinking about the location for the rock, I saw a light out of the corner of my eye. The light was off to my right and slightly behind me. It was now about 5 am, and too early for it to be from the rising sun. Also, the light was coming from the west, not the east, the opposite of a rising sun. I recall being startled enough to ask, "What was that?" I turned to look more directly at the light, and as I did, it began to approach me. The light was at ground level, and at a distance that seemed about a football field away. It appeared to be about 30 yards wide, but as it approached me, it narrowed to the width of my outstretched arms. It moved from wide to narrow—*just the opposite* of how light moves. As quickly as it approached me, it retreated. It did this twice. The light moved at a measurable speed—at a count of 1001, 1002, 1003, 1004—moving toward me and the same count moving away. Light docs not travel at a measurable speed to the human eye; its movement is instantaneous, but I could follow this light like you would follow a person walking. There was darkness between me and the light. It had a specific beginning and end, not all-encompassing as light normally is. It did not glow like a candle, and it wasn't bright like a headlight. I don't know how else to describe it other than I believed it was the light of God.

The past few hours had been filled with one emotional experience after another. I had been crying uncontrollably all night, and now I went to pieces again. I was crying so hard it was difficult to think and breathe and to stand up, but I had enough awareness that I knew I had to mark the spot where this experience had just occurred. There was a stick about 10 yards away, but I was afraid to move from the exact place I was standing, so I anchored the heel of my right foot and started to spin so I would make a visible mark on the ground. After I made the mark, I took my shoe off and placed it on the spot. I grabbed the stick and put it in the ground at the exact place I was standing when I saw the light.

I didn't understand the events of the night, but I said to myself, *Mike, you have one of two choices to make.* Option one was not to tell anyone about this. If I told others what had occurred, they might think I was crazy or lying. The safe option would be to not tell anyone and keep what occurred this night to myself. Option two was to walk off the hill and share this with anyone who would listen. If people thought I was crazy, I would be okay with that. It didn't take me more than a few seconds to decide that I was going to tell people about the Godly experiences I had that night. I walked off the hill, went into the house, took a shower, and went to work to see my art director. I had to get the contract ready to send to Roger.

I told my art director not to ask me any questions about what had occurred the night before or to ask what this was all about. I didn't have the time to get into that because we had to get the contract and the final document prepared and sent to Roger. I asked her to take the materials I had created and put them into a presentable format. When she was done, I would work with her to refine them. The 11 pages that were created the night before made up the contract. These documents included a signature/commitment page, organizational graphs, and giving plans. I also included photographs of my family because I had been instructed by God to include some information and photographs for each

Cloister location, and news and magazine articles about my business. Later, I reluctantly added biblical scripture that Ned Pelger insisted I include. The document in its finished form was 52 pages long. I refer to the signature/commitment page and the organizational graphs and giving plans as the "contract," and all 52 pages as the "document."

Getting the Signatures

I gave this information to my art director on Wednesday so she could design the graphics and add supporting information. I had promised Roger I would give him an answer about our partnership by Friday, so he needed to see the contract before our discussion could continue. I had been working on putting the final document together for about two hours when it struck me that there were signatures I had to get. Randy, Dennis, Ned, and Tom were as much a part of this as Roger and I were. Their signatures were critically important. I was very concerned about what they would think of me and extremely scared about asking them to sign the commitment. I thought, *What happens if any of these four people don't want to sign this?* They might think, *Mike has created a contract between God, Roger, and Mike. How can I testify that God is a part of this?* All the people I was asking to sign this, with the exception of Roger, were very spiritual people. Randy was a deacon in the Mennonite church. Dennis was a Methodist preacher. And Ned and Tom had deep and long-standing spiritual beliefs and were very well-versed in the teachings of the Bible. This was not something they would be casual about signing. At first, I thought if someone doesn't want to sign the commitment, I would find someone else who would. Then I realized this was not my contract. I didn't write this contract. This was God's contract. There was a reason these people were selected, and if they would not sign it, then there would be no partnership. If any one of the four didn't want to sign the commitment, then I could not move forward with my discussions with Roger. It was going to take courage on my part to ask them to do this.

I made copies of the signature/commitment page and went to see Ned first. I told him about Roger's proposal and that an amazing thing had happened to me. I did not get into any of the details about what had occurred the night the contract was created. I wanted Ned and the others to be a part of this because they had faith in me and they had faith in their personal beliefs. I didn't want them to sign this because I had convinced them that a miracle had occurred. I asked Ned to review the commitment I was asking him to make and to let me know if he would be willing to sign it. Then I went to see Dennis at his church and asked him the same thing. I did not pressure either of them. I wanted them to feel comfortable with what I was asking them to do. Next, I met with Randy. He had worked for me for only six weeks. I assured him there was a reason his name was selected, and that in my heart and mind he had no obligation to sign it because he worked for me. As with Dennis, I was a little embarrassed to ask Randy because we didn't know each other that well at the time. Randy agreed to take the commitment page home and talk it over with his family. He said that they made decisions as a family and that he would pray about this. Now it was out of my hands. If any of these three people said no, there would be no partnership with Roger. I decided I would send Tom a copy of the finished document at the same time I sent a copy to Roger. I planned to call Tom after he had time to review it. At this point, I had not met or spoken with him.

The following day, I visited with Ned and asked him what he decided. He told me that he prayed about it, and that God had made it very clear to him what he should do. He would sign the contract if some biblical verses were added to the document.

Ned emphasized this was God's request. I didn't anticipate or appreciate this because I was not directed to do this by God. How could I be certain that God had directed Ned? I decided that God would have let me know if this was inappropriate. I included the biblical verses, and Ned signed the commitment. What God added through Ned was the suggestion to read Philippians chapters 1 through 4, and verses from 1 and 2 Timothy and 1 Thessalonians. These additions appear on page 18 in the document. The last verse that was added holds deep personal importance to me. It is 2 Timothy 4:6-7 (Paul's words knowing that he will be executed soon):

"For I am already being poured out like a drink offering, and the time has come for my departure. I have fought the good fight, I have finished the race, I have kept the faith."

I felt like this was happening to me, like I was living that verse.

Next, I went to see Dennis. Reverend Dennis Snovel was a minister in the United Methodist Church. During his ministry, he had served as a pastor at five Methodist churches in Pennsylvania. I was particularly concerned that Dennis would have a problem signing the commitment because he was a minister. I had only recently joined his Hopeland United Methodist Church after attending a few introductory classes with Rhoda, which was a requirement to become members. I was troubled with two things Dennis said during these classes. One was that a gay lifestyle was not accepted in Methodist Christian beliefs, and the other was that God does not want us to work on the Sabbath, and for Christians that's Sunday. I didn't believe sexual orientation was a criterion for being a Christian; I believed we were all God's children. Also, I had to work on Sunday because of the nature of my business, even though this troubled me at times, just as others like hospital workers, police departments, and priests and ministers do. I did talk to Dennis about these concerns, and we worked through them, but I thought that he might have some issues with me because of that. We would briefly chat on Sundays after church, but I was always in a hurry to get to work. I was not yet close to Dennis, so I was not sure how he would react to my telling him that God had made him a part of a contract for a business venture I was about to get into. He said he understood my concerns, which he prayed about, and he was comfortable signing the commitment.

The next day, I met with Randy at work. I reassured Randy that I didn't want him to sign because he felt pressured. I wanted Randy to sign it only if he believed it was the right thing to do. Randy told me that he and his family prayed about it and that he was willing to sign the commitment. Randy shared with me that he believed in what God was capable of doing through individuals and organizations, and that he felt blessed to be a part of this.

I couldn't believe that these three people had the faith and trust in me to sign the commitment. What I was asking them to sign was very unusual. If I had any doubts about God guiding me in the creation of this contract, their support removed my doubt. To me, it was a Godly moment that I got their signatures, and that the faith of the three of them was this strong.

The document was ready to send to Roger and Tom. The final step was for them to sign the commitment page. It was Thursday, and I sent it overnight so it would arrive by the time I had promised to respond to Roger. This was a simple contract. The entire spiral-bound document I sent was 52 pages, including photos and background information, but the contract was a single signature/commitment page, plus the organizational charts and the giving plans.

The essence of the commitment page, to be signed by six people, was that we would keep God first in our partnership relationship. This was the part that was important to me. The traditional legal agreements would come later. If Roger agreed that we would allow God's wisdom and grace to guide our business dealings, then I knew that the other details could be worked out.

Up to this point, I had shared very few details with Rhoda, Dennis, Ned, and Randy about what had occurred the night God had guided me to write the Grace contract. I felt it was time to take them, step-by-step, through the events of that night.

On Friday, the day Roger received the document, I took Rhoda out to dinner at an Olive Garden Italian restaurant we both liked. I told her I had something very important to share with her. She wanted to know what it was, but I asked for her patience and said that I would tell her and show her what was on my mind the following morning. On Saturday morning, I put on the robe and loafers I wore the night the Godly experience had occurred, and woke Rhoda up at 5 am. She looked at me with sleepy curiosity. "Why can't you just tell me what this is about?" she sighed with a bit of frustration in her voice. She reluctantly got up and put on old sweat pants and a top, and we walked through the sequence of events. I started crying as soon as we started down the steps from our bedroom. We walked to the trophy room, and I told her about the writing of the contract. We sat on the porch, and I told her about the two times I was transformed into a childlike state. We walked up the hill to the rock, and we both knelt as I repeated the prayers I said that night. Then we sat on the front of the rock just as I had. We moved from the rock to where I saw the light, and I described to her the qualities of the light. Rhoda was not acknowledging anything. I was not sure what she was thinking when I told her what had occurred. It was overwhelming and a lot to grasp. She was very quiet, and that raised my fear that people were going to think that I had lost my mind. Rhoda told me afterward, "God appears in unexpected and mysterious ways if we are open to the possibility. I believe God was revealed to you."

I walked with my minister, Dennis, at 6 am on Monday. He had agreed to meet with me when we spoke after church the day before. I met Dennis as he parked his car in our driveway. I was once again dressed in my robe and loafers. I walked him through what had occurred that night, just as I did with Rhoda. When we knelt at the rock, Dennis joined me in reciting the Lord's Prayer and the 23rd Psalm. Much like Rhoda, Dennis was very quiet for the entire time other than when we prayed. After we walked off the hill, we went back into the trophy room, and I shared with Dennis some of the other Godly experiences that I have had in my life that I have written about in this book. This was the first time I had told Dennis about them. Dennis looked at me and said, "Mike, there is no doubt in my mind that you have had these experiences. I can only wish that I would have experienced 10 percent of what you have experienced." His remark was very important to me because I felt that he truly believed that something Godly had occurred. His remarks made me feel spiritually credible. I immediately responded to him, *"That's why your love for God is incredible. Your beliefs are based on faith, not because you have witnessed. I have no reason not to believe. I have witnessed God's grace."* My remark surprised me because it was so spontaneous, and I wasn't sure where that insight came from, but I believed very strongly that God's chosen people are people of faith. Dennis and I shook hands, and he left. I did learn sometime later that the Bible teaches that strength comes from faith, not from witness, and that's what I was trying to express to Dennis.

My experience with Ned was different than the others. Ned was not able to meet with me until Wednesday, and he wasn't willing to do it early in the morning. I tried to talk Ned into meeting me before sunrise because I felt that it helped re-create the experience. I was also concerned that later in the day we would be distracted by men working at the farm, and I didn't want them to see me crying. I couldn't get Ned to change the time, so we met midmorning, and I walked him through what had occurred that night. I was not wearing the robe and loafers when we took our walk as I did when I walked with Rhoda and Dennis. These walks were very emotional for me, as I relived the experience. By the time Ned and I had reached the spot where I saw the light, I was uncontrollably weeping, and I felt embarrassed in front of him, as I did with Rhoda and Dennis. I couldn't talk to Rhoda, Dennis, or Ned face-to-face, and I wondered what they were thinking about me and the incredible experience I was sharing with them. Did all three of them think I was losing my mind?

Ned was standing behind my right shoulder with his back facing the direction that the light came from when he said something that surprised me. Ned said, "Mike, there's zero doubt in my mind that this happened to you. I absolutely know that it did. You had a remarkable experience. God was with you!" Then Ned added, "For as great as what happened to you is, something equally bad is going to happen. Mike, you are going to be tested. Something bad is going to happen to you, your family, your health, or your wealth. Maybe you'll lose a loved one. I don't know, but I have very strong feelings about it." I heard what Ned said, but I passed over his comments like we pass over comments friends make that we don't take seriously. I didn't want to think about what he said, especially after this Godly experience had occurred. I didn't know it at the time, but I had early symptoms of a serious illness. Ned's prediction was about to come true.

I received an e-mail from Roger on November 23, 2004, two weeks after he received the document. A few days later we talked on the phone. He told me that our business philosophies were similar, but our religious beliefs were at opposite ends of the spectrum. He would not sign the Grace contract, because he did not believe in God, and he could not in good conscience enter into any agreement under false pretenses. I told Roger that a mutual belief in God was important to me, and if that belief did not exist, we could not be partners. We talked about the contract, but the enthusiasm had now cooled. Before we hung up, we agreed to take some time to think about everything before we decided to terminate our partnership discussion.

A few weeks after Roger told me he would not sign the contract, Randy and I made the four-hour drive to Washington, DC, to meet with Tom, Roger's friend. Tom lived in Canada and was in Washington on business. I had not heard from Tom after I sent him the document, so I called him and he agreed to meet me. Much like Roger, Tom was a very accomplished man, but I did not know this about Tom when I first met him.

Roger had told me that Tom was a very spiritual person, and I was hopeful that Tom could convince Roger to sign the contract. Tom was staying at an upscale hotel in downtown Washington. I believed the woman at the front desk knew Tom because of the way she spoke about him, and I got the impression that I was about to meet someone very special.

Tom came to greet Randy and me in the lobby. He was a middle-aged man with a conservative air about him. He escorted us to a modest room, very unlike the surroundings of the rest of the hotel. We talked for two hours, and Tom was very pleasant and attentive. I was still overwhelmed with what had occurred the night the contract was created, and I had trouble controlling my emotions. I tearfully told Tom about that night and how I was instructed by God to include his name. I reviewed my conversation with Roger after he received the finished document and declined to sign the contract. I believed Tom was willing to sign the contract, but absent Roger's signature, there was no point to pursue that now. Tom seemed surprised that Roger would not sign the contract, and he told me that he had been friends with Roger the better part of their lives and that he had no idea that he didn't believe in God.

Tom was very familiar with the Bible. During our visit, he referred to the Bible in the hotel room to draw parallels to my Godly experience and biblical verses. I had taken my grandfather's Bible with me on the trip. This Bible was given to me by my grandmother when my grandfather passed away, and it was very important to me. My grandfather had made handwritten notes in the Bible. He had underlined verses that were important to him, and he noted the birth dates of all his children. He even noted the day his son Eugene had died at birth. The Bible was something that I cherished. As Randy and I got ready to leave, I offered the Bible to Tom, thinking it was something that he would appreciate having with him during his time in Washington and for his trip back to Canada. I also thought the gesture would tell him something about me. I knew that he was a spiritual man from what Roger had told me about him, and I thought the Bible would be a symbol of how important the contract was to me. I didn't intend for Tom to keep the Bible, but I thought the gesture to take it with him would build trust between us. I told him to send it back to me when it was convenient for him. At first, he cordially declined to take it. I said I would leave it outside his hotel room door if he didn't accept my offer, so with a little laughter between us he accepted it with sincere words of thanks. I didn't get the Bible back after a few weeks, so I followed up with Tom to check the status. He said he wanted to visit with me and Rhoda at our farm to deliver it personally. He also expressed interest in walking through the experience I had the night the contract was created. To my disappointment, Tom never did visit, and two years after I gave the Bible to him, I got it back in the mail. I never did find out if Tom talked with Roger about our meeting, or if he tried to convince Roger to sign the contract.

Something Good, Something Bad

The night the Grace contract was created was my greatest Godly moment. I was pleased that I could relive that night when I walked Rhoda, Dennis, and Ned through the experience. However, the moment

Ned and I walked off the hill, Ned's prediction about something bad happening to me started to unfold. Within weeks, I got sick with what I thought was the flu, but what prompted me to seek medical help was a mark on my chest that was four inches in diameter and looked like a target. My son Elton thought this might be from a tick bite, and he mentioned Lyme disease. I was burning up with a fever and getting sicker by the day. I went to see my doctor, and he immediately suspected that I had Lyme disease. All the blood work that was done came back negative, but my doctor suggested we treat my condition as Lyme disease because the disease doesn't always show up in blood work. We tried antibiotics, but my health continued to deteriorate. We tried Lyme disease drugs, but nothing worked. My heart started to act erratically. I reached a point where I could hardly walk, and I had a number of serious falls on the steps in my farmhouse. I couldn't turn my neck. I couldn't think clearly, and I started to fall into depression. Dealing with my illness and depression was changing my personality. I would get into heated arguments with friends and loved ones, including Ned. Personal relationships, which had always been very important to me, were starting to deteriorate along with my health.

At times, I felt like I was going to die. Eventually, I was hospitalized and a heart monitor was installed, but my doctors could not figure out what was wrong with me, and my health continued to get worse. After trying multiple medicines to treat Lyme disease, my doctors decided to try one more medicine that they thought might be effective. Before I could start this new medicine, I had to be slowly taken off of lithium, which I had been using since 1988 to combat depression. A nurse came to the farm to give me the medicine. It was injected through a pic line that was installed in a vein in my arm and then went through my body and into my heart. The medicine looked like motor oil, and I wondered if I would live through this illness.

Within one month of stopping the lithium, I went into a state of deep depression. I felt like I was pushed off the Empire State Building. To get me out of my depression, I went through 14 electroconvulsive therapy treatments (ECT). With ECT, an electroshock triggers a seizure that can last up to three minutes and resets brain function. This occurred in an operating room. Electrodes were placed around my head, and I was given an injection that disabled my muscle and breathing functions. A machine kept me breathing. I had these treatments three times a week for more than a month, and they were brutal. I dreaded the thought of knowing high-voltage electricity was going to be sent through my brain. I always felt like I was hit with a sledgehammer after each treatment, even though I was asleep during the procedure. I also experienced severe memory loss, which is a side effect of the therapy. My business almost went bankrupt during the time I was sick. I was so emotionally distraught that I thought I was going to die. At times I felt that I wanted to die, but I never once questioned God's love or asked God, "Why did you put all of these challenges in my path?" I thought this might be the end of my life, but I decided if God was leading, I was going to follow. I was prepared to accept whatever God had planned for me. I thought the Bible verse Ned wanted me to include in the Grace Friendship and Partnership Contract document was coming true: *"For I am already being poured out like a drink offering, and the time has come for my departure. I have fought the good fight, I have finished the race, I have kept the faith."* I began to think the writing of the Grace Friendship and Partnership Contract was the completion of God's work for me on Earth.

I suffered with the illness for almost a year, and a very deep depression for six months of that year. At the depth of the depression, I could not function, and I felt that I was close to death. Every aspect of my life was affected. There wasn't a day that I was not in pain or emotional turmoil. This was the most difficult time of my life.

Rhoda was by my side every day I was sick. She worked full-time at the business while she cared for me. She took me to Hershey Medical Center (the Hershey of Hershey's chocolate and now formally known as Penn State Health Milton S. Hershey Medical Center) for my ECT treatments. I didn't want to go, but Rhoda refused to allow me to miss them because she was hoping these treatments were my way back to a normal life. She worked closely with Ned, Randy, Jim, and a new president and chief financial officer during the construction of the Reading facility. She also attended difficult and often combative township meetings during the construction. Everyone was scared and concerned about me during this time. Randy told me Rhoda would constantly say to him, "Just get it opened. We need to start generating cash!" She was determined she was going to get me, our family, and the business through this difficult time. She monitored me closely and made sure I was never left alone because she was fearful of what I might do to myself. She even took my guns and ammunition out of the house. I didn't think about committing suicide, but she wasn't taking any chances.

As I started to recover from the ECT treatments, Rhoda would take me around to the facilities so I could gradually ease my way back into work. She wanted to make sure I didn't go back to work before I was physically and mentally ready. Rhoda's faith was being tested as much as mine during this time. I often ask Rhoda how she managed all this. She always replies, "I prayed a lot. I sometimes felt alone, but I knew we were not alone. God was with us every step of the way." With God's love, and Rhoda's love and help, we got through the ordeal. After the ECT treatments, my health began to rebound, and I started to regain my memory. It was never definitively determined that I had Lyme disease. The symptoms of my illness have not re-occurred.

I spent a lot of time with Ned during my illness, asking him to help me understand the experiences I had the night the contract was created. We also talked about what prompted him to make his comment about something bad happening to me, even though he never said, "I told you something bad would happen to you." I often wondered if it was Ned speaking or God speaking through him.

Ned was also the project manager for the building of the Reading car wash. The project was a huge undertaking. We believed it was the largest car wash of its type in the world. The complex was 44,000 square feet under roof, on more than seven acres of land, and built at an investment of 12 million dollars. It would eventually employ 125 people. The future of my company depended on the success of this new location, so Ned and I would meet as many as three times a week to talk about the project. After we were finished talking about the project, the conversation would inevitably turn to discussing God, the creation of the contract, and my illness. I was desperately looking for some insight into why I would be so blessed, and then so physically and mentally ill that I almost lost everything. Ned even arranged a meeting that included my friend Paul Martin to discuss my erratic behavior, a meeting that got a little heated. I was constantly asking Ned to help me interpret what was happening to me. I have never stopped talking to Ned about those times. Ned has explained to me that there are many references in the Bible about how blessings are followed by tests. Examples of these references can be found in writings about Paul, David, and Job. Knowledge of these biblical references is what prompted him to alert me that something challenging would follow my experience of creating the Grace Friendship and Partnership Contract. Randy also offered some insight on why I got ill. I learned from Randy that what happened to me is referred to in the Bible as a Refiner's Fire. A Refiner's Fire follows a calling by God to do something spiritually meaningful, like writing the Grace Friendship and Partnership Contract. After the blessing of being called by God, I was tested—put through the fire— so I could emerge from this challenge stronger and with more spiritual clarity. That's exactly what happened to me.

Ned's comment about something bad occurring was lost on me at first. I'm not sure if Ned totally understood how his prediction and my illness were so connected. I didn't think about it very much until I was sick. I now find it amazing that his prediction came true. I have told Ned numerous times, "Don't you ever say that to me again." We nod at each other knowingly and just smile.

I also asked Ned for his insight on the word *grace,* and what he could share with me from biblical teachings about the light I saw. Prior to my experience with the Grace contract, the word *grace* meant very little to me. God brought the power of the word to my attention when I was instructed to call what was created the Grace Friendship and

Partnership Contract. I wondered why the contract wasn't called Mike's Contract or Mike and Roger's Contract. Why not something more common or businesslike? It didn't make sense to me until Ned helped me to understand the spiritual significance of the word. I have since used the word when I created Grace For Vets, and I named my property in Lancaster County Grace Farm after my experience on the hill. I have named my farm in New Zealand Grace Farm 2017. This book is about God's grace—something that I feel applies to me, and I am proud to honor God by writing about that. Even today, when I hear the words *grace* or *light* in church sermons, my heart is touched and I am sometimes brought to tears of joy. Sometimes I cry so hard that I have to walk outside. The song "Amazing Grace" does the same thing to me, as does Leonard Cohen's "Hallelujah" when I hear the lyric about "somebody who's seen the light." Ned is very well-versed in scripture. He is the only person I personally know who has read the Bible from cover to cover multiple times. He passionately explained to me that the word *grace* is widely used in the Bible, as is the image of light, as in "God is light." Ned taught me that the word *grace* is a very meaningful word to God, and that any time God wanted to illuminate an important message or teaching, God used the image of light. Ned was not surprised that my Godly experience included the word *grace* and the vision of a Godly light. His explanation brought me to tears. In fact, I fell to pieces, but his words have proven to be very helpful, comforting, and truly amazing to me.

I didn't know the Bible. I had never been taught the Bible. I am unable to read the Bible, but numerous examples of things that were written in the Bible were happening to me. It was overwhelming. Talking with Ned was always a special time for me. I owe Ned a debt of gratitude for helping me understand what had occurred the night that the Grace contract was created and the illness that followed. I also owe Rhoda and Sister Rosemary, whom you'll read about later in this book, my sincere thanks for teaching me about God's love during this time of my life.

Randy and I never took the walk. I decided at the time that it was just too much to put on an employee who had worked for me for only a short period of time. I was grateful that he signed the contract, and I felt that was enough to ask of him. I did talk to Randy in some detail about what had occurred that night. I answered his questions, and he offered his insights based on his religious experiences and training. Randy told me he believed that something Godly had occurred the night the contract was written. He told me he could feel it, even though I had offered no specifics when I first told him about it. He told me it was this strong feeling that he had, and his trust in me, that made him comfortable signing the contract. Randy heard about the experience a second time, this time in depth, when he traveled with me to meet Tom in Washington, DC.

I am absolutely positive that what happened to me for a year following the experience of creating the Grace Friendship and Partnership Contract was a test. God wanted to know if I would keep my faith when Roger didn't sign the contract. I wanted that relationship to work. I know that it would have been a very beneficial one for both of us. Roger was a special person with extraordinary financial resources, but I held firm on my belief that we had to partner with God, and Roger did not want to do that. I kept my faith and didn't give in. God has tested my faith many times throughout my life. Every test God has given me has grown more intense. The ultimate test was whether I would keep my faith when my health, wealth, and happiness were being stripped away. These were difficult tests of faith, but I emerged physically, mentally, and spiritually stronger. This strength would be challenged when a second partnership opportunity with Roger arose.

Building the Reading Car Wash

I was disappointed that a partnership with Roger did not work out, but I was at peace knowing that God had shown me that the partnership would not have been the best thing for me and my family. The Grace Friendship and Partnership Contract between God, Roger, and me centered entirely on building the circular car washes Roger had designed. There had been no discussion between Roger and me about partnering, or providing financing, on the car washes I owned, including the one that was being built in Reading. When Roger decided not to sign the Grace Friendship and Partnership Contract, I thought my business dealings with him had come to an end, even though we did stay in touch with each other over the next year and a half.

I turned my attention to finishing the building of the new Reading location, which I planned to open in the winter of 2005 to 2006. This was a huge undertaking, as I explained earlier. It was during this long period of construction that the illness I had battled throughout 2005 caught up with me. I was first hospitalized at the Ephrata Hospital for an unknown illness, before I went to the Hershey Medical Center to start the ECT treatments. Every day up to that point, I was finding it difficult, if not impossible, to do my job. I was doing everything that I could to keep the Reading project moving forward, but my deteriorating physical and mental health was making it impossible for me to stay on top of construction management. To complicate matters, I had made some high-level personnel changes at Cloister in 2005. They included replacing my VP of finance and hiring a president. I needed help to run my business because I was getting sicker and weaker by the day, and I felt I couldn't do my job competently because of my illness.

We had also significantly underestimated the cost of the Reading project. This was because of additional restrictions and compliances that the township had required us to make that were not part of our planning when we started construction. There were also some changes that I felt we had to make once construction was under way that we had not budgeted. We were 70 percent through construction and had already invested $10 million in the project and were almost out of the money we had borrowed to build the Reading facility. I was under tremendous stress and still not feeling my best. Despite the condition I was in, we had to figure out a way to finish the project and keep the business running. We were able to finish and open the Reading facility by using some creative money management, and by trying to use, as much as possible, cash generated by our three other locations. This was a short-term fix that left us desperately short of funds to manage all four of our locations after the Reading facility was opened. Contractors and suppliers were knocking on our door for money, and our lenders were deeply concerned. Rhoda and I did not take a paycheck for many months, and employee wages were cut 5 percent. The sacrifice Cloister employees made helped us to get past our financial problems, and I will always be thankful to them. It's also important to acknowledge that all the contractors worked with me, too. I stayed in touch with them to keep them informed of payment status. Often the past due amounts were large sums of money. Many of them told me not to worry about paying them immediately. They trusted me and had faith in me, and they knew that they would get paid. I was very grateful for their kindness and understanding. Every contractor who worked on the Reading project was eventually paid in full.

Arranging the financing on the Reading project was difficult to start with, so asking the lender for more money was not likely to happen. I understood the bank's concerns. A lot of attention was paid to the appearance of Cloister Car Wash locations. They were expensive to build and to landscape. Car washes are also single-use buildings. Banks are reluctant to invest in properties that have limited uses. Car washes are also at the mercy of the weather, and banks don't like unknowns. When you consider all these factors, banks will be very conservative with the amount of money they are willing to lend to build a car wash. Our budget was very tight to start with, and now we were way over budget. On top of this, I had two new executives, Charley, the new president, and Steve, the new VP of finance, to work with. When I went to see the bank, they were not interested in investing more money in the Reading project. I was disappointed, but not surprised, that they were not willing to do this. I believe this was because they knew about Roger and his interest in partnering with me and that he would be able to put money into the business. I was always appreciative that they provided the original funding for the Reading project. We had to find another source of additional financing, and we had to find it quickly.

I had hired Charley as president of Cloister in the fall of 2005. I had known him for many years, and he was someone I trusted. I knew that he would watch out for my interests and the interests of my family. He had his hands full. He did not have car wash experience, and he did not have a strong background in finance. He was a logical, fair, and clear-thinking executive with a strong production background. I thought that he was a perfect fit to run the business while I recovered from my illness and to work with me when I returned. Charley started to work with Steve, who joined Cloister a few months before Charley, to look for additional funding to keep the business going. I was so sick at this point that I couldn't be of much help to Charley. When he would talk to me to keep me up-to-date, or to get my opinion on something, I could offer very little input. I would also quickly forget what we discussed because of the ECT treatments.

I don't know how Charley and Steve found out about Roger. It's possible that the bank told them about Roger and suggested they contact him. More than a year had passed since Roger and I had ended our conversation about a partnership. I might have told Charley and Steve about him and then forgotten the conversation. I doubt that I would have suggested Roger as a source of financing because of his reaction to the Grace Friendship and Partnership Contract. I would have wanted a similar, simple contract between God, Roger, and me if Roger was loaning us money, and I would have had no reason to think that he would do that.

Charley didn't know the details of my previous discussions with Roger, but somehow he found out that Roger had money and an interest in the car wash business, so he contacted him to discuss a loan. Roger was willing to loan us money. Roger, Charley, and Steve worked out a loan package that included two installments. The first part was for $1,250,000 to use for operations and to pay off past due contractors and suppliers. We would receive this money in the spring of 2006. The second part, due to be received a month after the first installment, was for $750,000. There was also a stipulation that the loans could be converted to Cloister Car Wash stock and Roger would become a minority owner of Cloister. The $2 million was the amount we needed to get Cloister back on solid financial footing. Charley gave Roger and his lawyers the go-ahead to draft the loan and stockholder agreements. I'm sure Charley told me about the agreements with Roger, but I was in no condition to carefully think about them, or to consider the ramifications of giving up some ownership in my business. I was so sick at this time that I felt I might die. I must have given my okay to make the deal with Roger, but I still don't have any recollection of that. The ECT treatments affected my memory that badly. Our bank was supportive of this deal. I had mentioned to the bank that I had met Roger and that he was interested in getting involved in business with me. I had told the bank that Roger was well-established and well-funded, and I believe that was a factor for them turning down my request for additional financing. They wanted me to get financial help from Roger because that would protect their investment without any additional lending from the bank.

I was starting to feel better. The ECT treatments at Hershey Medical Center certainly helped. I also believe God's mercy was freeing me from my illness, and my test was ending. The "Refiner's Fire" Randy spoke about was over. With Rhoda's help and love, I got myself back to work, even though I was still extremely exhausted and not at my best. The loss of my long-term memory was a big problem for me. My first priority, now that the Reading wash was fully operational, was to get a handle on the financial condition of the business, which was much worse than I realized. People had been hiding that from me so my illness and worries would not get worse. Rhoda was carrying this burden on her shoulders.

I reviewed the agreements we had with Roger with my new VP of Finance, Julie, whom I had hired to replace Steve. Roger had already invested the first part of the package—$1,250,000. I sat at my desk staring at the complex, one-inch-thick document that was very difficult for me to read because of my dyslexia. I understood enough of it to know that it was not a deal that made sense for me and Cloister. What we needed was the same simple one-page document that I had proposed before—a Friendship and Partnership Contract between God, Roger, and me. The legal documents would be the details of the agreement, but Roger would need to agree that God would be part of our partnership, and I knew from our previous experience that he would not agree to that. We needed to find a way to pay back what Roger had already loaned us, and we needed to find a way to survive without the second installment of $750,000. I told Julie that I could not live with the agreements we had with Roger. We had to find the money somewhere else. I remember the shock on her face. We had been turned down by our bank and many other lenders for additional financing, and here I was saying "no" to the only source of financing that was being offered. The business was in trouble—bankruptcy was a possibility—but I was not going to partner with Roger unless the relationship included God. We were out of money, and creditors were calling daily, but I was not going to sacrifice my beliefs and my trust in God for money.

Now that I was back running the business, I decided to terminate my contract with Charley at a significant expense to the company. I had agreed to pay him a year's wages if our contract was terminated early. We didn't need both of us to run the business, and I felt it was just better to move on. We paid Charley everything we owed him per the terms and conditions of the contract we had agreed to. It was a significant amount of money, and it put added pressure on the financial difficulties we already had. I remember Charley coming to the office every payday to pick up his check. I don't think he believed we would get through our financial difficulties without filing for bankruptcy. Charley and I parted ways on friendly terms, and we remained friends until his death in 2016.

I called Roger and told him my decision. I still felt that Roger and I would make a dynamic team. We were out-of-the-box thinkers, and our different backgrounds and skills included the ingredients for a powerful alliance. We could have accomplished a lot together. However, there was that missing piece—the acceptance of God as our partner. I summarized my feelings when I spoke to Roger by saying that the simple contract I had proposed a year earlier included accepting God as our partner. He had rejected this. Unless we had that same understanding now, the terms and conditions of his offer to help Cloister get through its financial difficulties were not acceptable to me. The complex loan and stockholder agreements that he had sent us made it clear to me that what he was proposing did not include God. Roger was very disappointed, if not angry. A few days after I turned down his offer, I received a phone call from Roger's chief financial officer to let me know that they expected me to reimburse them for the legal, accounting, and personal expenses they had incurred to draft the agreements. I did feel an obligation to pay for this. The cost was tens of thousands of dollars. The burden of this expense made me think again about accepting Roger's money, but I knew it was not the right thing to do. I was not going to give in to this temptation. We paid the expenses even though we were desperately short on cash.

After I turned down Roger's proposal, I contacted Marathon Group, a business broker in Reading, who helped us find a lender. Marathon talked with a number of companies before they found Business Loan Express, who consolidated our loans in early 2007. The new loan was for $14 million. Our bank was shocked when I told them about this. They came back with a loan proposal after turning us down earlier. I was so annoyed at them that I declined their offer. I find it remarkable that we couldn't find a lender before Roger's loan. Then, I made the decision that Roger's proposal was not right for us, and a lender appeared to refinance the business, including paying back Roger. God was watching over me once again. The loan got us on sound financial footing, and it allowed me to get back to running the business. A few years later, I was able to refinance Cloister's loan package at a much more competitive interest rate. We were once again financially stable, making a profit, and servicing our debts.

I was fully recovered from my illness by now. The Reading wash was generating cash flow which, in addition to the new loan, helped to remove the financial pressure. On the day we paid off Roger in March of 2007, he came to the Reading car wash. We stood side by side in the area we called Customerland, making small talk and watching cars move through the interior clean building. I know that both of us were disappointed that two opportunities at a partnership had not worked out. I followed Roger outside to say goodbye to him. Our conversation was very awkward, but we shook hands and wished each other well. I'll never forget the look in Roger's eyes. It was a look of acceptance that something good had slipped away, even though neither one of us was at fault. It was just not meant to be. I suspect I had the same look in my eyes. I didn't hear from Roger again until the spring of 2017. I had contacted him to let him know I was writing this book. I must acknowledge that the short-term loan Roger made to Cloister helped the company get out of financial trouble, and I will always be appreciative of that.

When Roger loaned Cloister money and proposed a partnership that included ownership in Cloister Car Wash, I rejected his proposal because he was still not willing to accept God as our business partner. I believe I was tested this second time to see if I would stay true to my belief that any partnership had to be between God, Roger, and me. I had the courage to walk away, even though I had not fully recovered from my illness and stood face-to-face with losing my business. My health did fully recover, and my business flourished. I believe this occurred because I put God first and I kept my faith. I had the courage to turn down a proposal that I knew would not work for me, even though my business was desperate for money.

The experience of creating the Grace Friendship and Partnership Contract, including everything that led to its creation and everything that followed, is the greatest of my Godly experiences to date. I often use the analogy: "It was my Super Bowl of Godly experiences."

The contract had a simple one-page commitment. The essence of the commitment was that the six people who were asked to sign the document would work for a common cause, a common good—*and put God first*. If we did that, we would be successful in business and every other aspect of our lives. That page, the heart and soul of the document, was followed by supporting charts and explanatory text, including a giving plan. The giving plan outlined how the gifts God would give me and my family would be used to help others—to positively change lives everywhere. A great deal of faith was required to believe that making significant personal financial sacrifices would not be a burden on my family. I trusted God that these sacrifices would be a path to God's grace. We demonstrate similar faith when we follow the teachings of the Bible, or any religious texts, even when we don't fully understand or agree with what they are instructing us to do.

The experience of creating the Grace Friendship and Partnership Contract, along with everything else that occurred that night, changed my life like no other Godly experience. I was tested, as were the others who were involved. Our trust in each other was tested. Our willingness to stand by our beliefs was tested. Our faith in God and in God's wisdom was tested. Ultimately, the experience made me, Rhoda, and the others who signed the contract spiritually stronger.

I am reminded once again of my friend Paul Martin's favorite quote: "Let go and let God!" Accept that God loves you and watches over you. I believe that letting go and letting God has changed my life forever. I also believe it will do the same for you.

Top: *Mike's friends at the Carmelite Monastery in Terre Haute, Indiana*

Bottom: *Front view of the monastery's chapel*

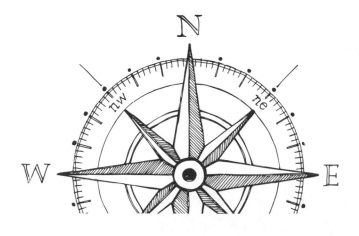

XII.

Carmelite Nuns

In the last chapter, I wrote that on the Sunday Roger first visited the Lancaster car wash, I had to leave early to look at a property in Reading, Pennsylvania. I was thinking about a fourth Cloister location, and I wanted to walk the property again before I made the commitment to buy the land. I had told the seller I would let him know my decision by Monday.

I arrived in Reading with about a half hour of daylight remaining before it would be too dark to walk the property. My cell phone rang, and I looked to see who was calling because I didn't want to get into a lengthy phone call. It was my dear friend and fellow car wash operator Bill Barclay from

Springfield, Missouri. Bill rarely called me, and I felt I had to take his call, so I found a large rock to sit on and answered the phone.

There was the usual warm greeting from Bill. We spent a few minutes in friendly small talk, and then Bill told me that he had been thinking about me and that he was calling about an incredible thing that God had done for him. He started by saying that I had never preached to him and had never brought up God's name. Yet, he always knew that I had a special relationship with God, and he could feel this when he was in my presence. Because of this, Bill felt that I would want to hear his story. It was getting darker, and I knew this wasn't going to be a short phone call, but I was intrigued to hear what was on his mind.

Bill told me that he had been trying to sell his car wash for years, but he couldn't find a buyer. Next, he told me that his wife, Jan, had been told that she had terminal cancer. "I was desperate and feeling totally up against it," Bill sighed.

Bill told me that he had needed someone to talk to, so he made a phone call to Bill Dahm, a mutual friend and a large car wash operator in the Midwest. During their phone call, Bill Dahm mentioned that his cousin, Sister Rosemary, was a Carmelite nun living in a monastery in Terre Haute, Indiana. He offered to call his cousin's monastery and put in a prayer request to ask the nuns to pray for Bill Barclay and Jan. Bill Dahm mentioned that he knew the nuns' prayers had made miracles happen for others, and he believed very strongly that this was worth doing. He told Bill Barclay that the nuns' prayers "could move mountains." There was a short pause on the phone, and then Bill Barclay told me, "My wife is free of cancer, and I sold my business for more money than I ever dreamed of!" Tears started running down my face, not just because of the positive outcome, but also because Bill thought enough of me, and my relationship with God, to want to let me know about this. I was joyful inside after hearing his story. I believe that all prayers are heard, but not all prayers are answered. We pray that God's will is done, and then we must accept the outcome. I was so happy that Bill's outcome was exactly what he had prayed for. Sometimes prayers do move mountains.

By now, it was dark outside. I was not going to be walking the property that night. I was on the phone so long that I looked at the battery indicator and saw that there was zero battery life left. I thought that it was strange that my phone didn't go dead even though we talked for another 10 minutes. I told Bill how wonderful and amazing his good news was. Bill said to me, "I felt so good about the prayers that I sent the Carmelite nuns a donation." When he told me the amount, I immediately decided I was going to make a modest donation, too. My friend had just told me that he believed the nuns' prayers had saved his wife's life, and he sold his business for more money than he ever dreamed he would, and I felt I had to acknowledge this miracle with a donation of my own. Had Bill not mentioned his donation, I would not have given this a second thought. My donation set in motion my friendship with the Carmelite nuns, and I believe the sequence of events—Bill's call, his telling me about the miracles, his donation, and my donation—was God's plan. I believe it was a Godly moment. Bill and I gave to the nuns because we wanted to, not because we felt an obligation. I don't believe God judges people by their generosity, but by the kindness of their hearts. Rich or poor, we can give thanks to God in many different ways. I asked Bill for the address of the nuns' monastery. I indicated that I might want to send in a prayer request myself. He faxed me the address the next day.

I wrote a letter to Sister Rosemary and enclosed a check. I told her that I knew her cousin, Bill Dahm, and his family. I said that Bill Barclay had told me about the miracles, that he and Jan were dear friends, and that I was so thankful for the nuns' prayers that I wanted to make a donation to thank God for the Barclays' good fortune. I never expected to hear back from Sister Rosemary or anyone else at the monastery, but my donation triggered correspondence between Sister Rosemary and me. One of her letters said that if I was ever in Terre Haute, she would love to meet me. This led to the most spiritually gratifying relationship of my life.

I first went to see the nuns on August 7, 2005. They also refer to themselves as sisters, but I will refer to them as nuns. Up to that point, I had no experience with nuns, and I don't recall ever seeing a nun. I did have an idea of how a nun dressed based on photographs and pictures in magazines I had seen. My exposure to Catholicism was limited to discussions I had over the years with friends who were Catholic, and the occasional Catholic wedding I would attend. I am a practicing Methodist, and I knew little or nothing about the history of the Catholic Church or how their religious services or practices differed from other branches of Christianity. I did believe that nuns were very religious and dedicated their lives to God, but I knew and understood little more than that.

I had exchanged a few letters and e-mails with Sister Rosemary before I went to see her. We had never talked on the phone. Rhoda and I had planned to go see her together, but schedule conflicts came up and Rhoda couldn't make the trip because of her workload at Cloister. I didn't want to go without Rhoda. I kept thinking about what I was going to do in the presence of nuns. What would I talk to them about? I was uneasy about this trip, but I felt drawn and compelled to go, so I decided to make the trip by myself.

I didn't schedule a visit with Sister Rosemary. I planned to make the 15 hour trip without her knowing that I was coming, and without any idea of what I was going to do when I got there. I just wanted to meet her. I packed a bag I called the Cloister Bag to give to her as a gift. I didn't know what to talk to a nun about, so I took things about my business. The bag included items we sold, used, or gave away at the car wash, including window cleaner, air fresheners, T-shirts, caps, aprons the greeters wore, an employee handbook, and literature. I recall thinking about just taking only one gift bag, and for a reason I can't explain, the number 12 came into my head. I decided I would take 12 of these Cloister bags with me. I didn't think I had more of these bags in inventory, but when I went back to the storage room and rummaged around, I found exactly 11 more bags. I filled all 12 bags with identical items and put them in my pick-up truck. Why I felt I needed twelve gift bags was a mystery to me. I just had the feeling once again that I was being guided to do this.

I left around 6:30 pm for the trip to Terre Haute. I planned to drive halfway, sleep an hour or two in the truck, and arrive the next morning. If Sister Rosemary could see me, I thought that we might visit for a few hours. If she couldn't see me, maybe I could meet some of the other nuns, or at minimum, tour the monastery. I planned to drive back to Lancaster County after what I thought would be a short visit at the monastery.

I arrived at the monastery around 10 am local time and stayed in the parking lot for a while, wondering what I was doing there. The setting was very intimidating. The monastery was a beautiful building, perched on a hilltop on property located a few miles outside the main area of Terre Haute. There were a few cars parked in the large parking lot that was located in front of the main entrance to the chapel. When I looked up the stone stairway that leads to the entrance, I could see the chapel located to my right. From this spot, I couldn't tell how large the complex was or what the property behind the main entrance looked like.

I still didn't know what I was going to do or talk

about if Sister Rosemary could see me. I again questioned what I was doing there. I thought that making this trip was crazy, and I should turn around and go back home. I tried to convince myself that leaving would be okay since no one knew that I was coming to visit.

I had the phone number you would call if you wanted to make a prayer request, but I had no other phone number. When I called, Sister Rosemary answered the phone, but she did not introduce herself and I had no idea it was her. I said hello, introduced myself, and told her that I was calling for Sister Rosemary. There was a pause, and then she asked me to wait a few seconds while she removed her headset. She asked me to repeat myself, and then she excitedly said, "That's me, that's me. I can't believe it's you, Michael. I'm rarely on the switchboard!" It was certainly a coincidence that she was on the phone that day, and I thought afterward if I had not left as early as I did the day before, I would have missed her. I cautiously added, "You're really not going to believe this: I'm sitting in your parking lot, hoping that I can come in and meet you." I was very pleased with the warm reception that I got, because Sister Rosemary wasn't expecting me. She told me that she would be able to meet with me at noon and asked me to come back then. I went to a Bob Evans restaurant to get something to eat, and I noticed that time was flying by because it was already 11:50. I raced to finish my meal and drove back to the monastery an hour before Sister Rosemary was expecting me. I had forgotten to set my watch back an hour to central time.

When I arrived back at the monastery, I was again taken by how beautiful it was. It was intimidating, but it also had a warm and welcoming aura about it. I knew in my soul that I was about to enter a special place. I walked up a flight of stone steps, passed through a heavy wooden door, and entered a beautiful foyer where I expected to meet Sister Rosemary. It was humbling to stand in this foyer. It was that spiritual. I could see inside the small chapel that was to the right when I entered the foyer. Straight ahead, at eye level, there was an 18- by 18-inch wooden door that was behind decorative wooden grillwork. To my left was a hallway that led to what I thought were probably meeting or work rooms. After a few moments, the small door opened, and I could see a nun's face through the grillwork. She said, "Hello," and asked if she could help me. I asked her if she was Sister Rosemary, but she was not. I was an hour early because of my time zone mix-up, but the nun who greeted me quickly found Sister Rosemary and told me that she was available to meet with me in the "Speak Room." I immediately thought to myself, "What is a Speak Room?" I was instructed to walk down a short hallway that was softly lit and beautifully but simply decorated with paintings and religious items. The Speak Room was through the first door on my left. I was about to embark on an experience that would profoundly impact my life.

The Speak Room was a small room, around 15 feet by 15 feet. It was called the Speak Room because it was where visitors went to talk with the nuns. There were a few living–room type chairs and other pieces of simple furniture placed along the walls. I was sitting on one of three padded chairs located at the front of the room. The chairs faced a wall about three feet high, and 20 inches thick, that extended the width of the room. Above the wall was a simple curtain. My first impression was that there was a stage behind the curtain. I waited for 10 minutes or so, expecting that Sister Rosemary would come into the room where I was sitting to greet me. The curtains slowly opened from my left, and I noticed ornamental grillwork about two feet above the wall. The room on the other side of the low wall was about the same size as the room I was in, with 15 to 20 wooden chairs facing me. This room was much more austere than the room I was sitting in. There was no way that I could see to get from my side of the wall to the other side.

When the curtains were fully opened, I was greeted by Sister Rosemary, who was sitting off to my right on the other side of the wall. She had a huge smile on her face, and I could sense how pleased she was that I was there. She was a petite woman. I couldn't see all of her face because of the brown habit she wore, but I could tell she was beautiful, with sparkling eyes and unblemished skin. We enjoyed some small talk like you would have with a friend you hadn't seen for a while but had known for a long time. This made me feel very comfortable in an environment that was totally foreign to me. She expressed surprise when I told her that I made the long trip from home just to meet her. She thought I was in Terre Haute on business. After a short time, we both moved our chairs close to the dividing wall so that we were about four feet away from each other, and face-to-face. Sister Rosemary asked me questions about my family, my personal interests, and my business. She was particularly interested in where the name "Cloister" came from. I told her the car wash was named Cloister Car Wash when I bought the business. I was afraid to change the name for fear of losing customers. I also shared with her that I thought about changing the name because I was afraid I would forget how to spell it because of my dyslexia, but wisely decided to keep the name Cloister. The name had spiritual connotations. The Cloister Foundation, located in Ephrata, Pennsylvania, is within walking distance of my first car wash. It is the historical site of a religious sect that dates back to the 1700s.

We talked about me for maybe an hour, and then our conversation turned to my Godly experiences. This conversation started like it always did— naturally and comfortably, without anything in particular prompting it. When I went to see Sister Rosemary, I did not plan on telling her about these experiences. But there I was, telling her about all the experiences I had from my accident in the Army through meeting Roger and creating the Grace Friendship and Partnership Contract. When I told others about these experiences, I would share one or two and not go into much detail. I went into detail with Sister Rosemary, and this was the first time I had ever told anyone about all of my experiences. We talked for hours, and I frequently got very emotional. Time flew by, and I was surprised when I noticed it was now late afternoon. Then, all of a sudden, Sister Rosemary started to shake and she said, "Just wait right here, please wait here," and she got up and left the room. I was happy for the break. I had been crying a lot, and I felt very exhausted. She came back a few minutes later with another nun, who introduced herself as Mother Anne. Mother Anne was older than Sister Rosemary, and she was the head of the monastery. She carried herself as a person of authority, but she was very pleasant, and I immediately sensed she had a warm heart. She made me feel comfortable just as Sister Rosemary did. Mother Anne sat down in the chair next to Sister Rosemary, and Sister Rosemary said to me, "Michael, please tell Mother Anne exactly what you told me."

I was very emotional and not sure where to start my conversation with Mother Anne. I thought because of the time I should pick up with my experience with the writing of the Grace contract. "No," Sister Rosemary said, "please start from the beginning." I questioned Sister Rosemary about starting over because I knew this would take hours. She insisted that I tell Mother Anne everything that I had told her. I went through all my Godly experiences again, and both nuns listened intently. By the time I was finished, it was around 8 pm, and I was emotionally drained—literally wiped out. Sister Rosemary must have been exhausted, too. I could sense that what I had talked about had the attention of the nuns. Mother Anne asked me if I could come back the following day at 9 am to spend more time with them. My original intention, and what I had told Rhoda, was to spend a few hours with Sister Rosemary, and maybe some time looking around the monastery, and then drive back to Lancaster County.

I agreed to come back the next day. I wanted to come back. The experience of talking so personally with Sister Rosemary and Mother Anne was overwhelming, yet joyous. I found a motel room nearby, got something to eat, and crashed.

I arrived at the monastery the following morning at a few minutes before 9 am and was instructed to go to the Speak Room. Sister Rosemary and Mother Anne were waiting for me. I could sense that they were eager to talk more about the Godly experiences that we had discussed the day before. They had many questions for me. I could see from the written material they had with them that they had prepared these questions from notes that they took as we spoke the day before. The questions were very thoughtful, intense, personal, and probing. Their manner was still very friendly, but they were also serious. I wouldn't say that I felt on trial, but clearly the nuns were trying to ascertain the truthfulness and validity of what I had told them. Between the questions about my experiences, they would ask me questions about my family, business, and personal interests. Some of the questions were the same questions that they asked the day before. I'm sure they wanted to see if my answers were consistent. This was both intimidating and stimulating. The day was very emotional, but it did pass very quickly. Before I knew it, it was 6 pm. I thought my time with the nuns was coming to an end, but Mother Anne, with a smile on her face and a businesslike tone in her voice, said, "Michael, can you come back tomorrow morning?" I thought, "You've got to be kidding." I was physically and emotionally exhausted, and I didn't know what to say to Rhoda about why I was extending a one-day trip to three days. I was also intrigued and flattered with the nuns' interest in me and my Godly experiences. I rarely talked to anybody about my experiences, and I had never gone into such depth as I had with the nuns, so I agreed to spend another day with them.

The next morning I decided to attend a 7:30 am Mass before I met with Sister Rosemary and Mother Anne to continue our conversations. This daily service is open to the public. I had never attended a Catholic Mass, so I didn't know what to expect. I usually sit in the back when I go to church at home, but that day I went to the front of the chapel and sat in the second row on the left, at the far left of the row. The chapel was simple, yet stunningly beautiful, and more spiritual than any place of worship I had ever been in. It was small compared to churches I was familiar with. I estimate it sat 100 people, maybe a few more. All of the 30 or so people who attended the Mass were sitting behind me. The priest was standing on an elevated altar, and behind him was a curtain. The curtain opened to reveal the nuns, who were seated behind a wrought-iron gate that separated them from the rest of the chapel. They sat in a U-shape, with the center of the U facing the front of the church. I was so moved by the spirituality of the setting that I started to cry. During the service, I sat with my head forward, and I cried so hard that the stone floor at my feet was wet with my tears. I am not exaggerating; the area that was wet was six inches in diameter. I had never cried that hard in my life. It was a constant stream of tears. I didn't cry because of what was being said; I was just that taken by the moment, my surroundings, the intense emotions of the previous two days, and the overwhelming presence of God that I felt inside me. During the service, I knelt and stood with everyone else. In my Methodist church we do stand occasionally but we don't kneel, so that was very unusual for me, and I felt uncomfortable at times. I frequently glanced to my right to see what other people were doing. I was just trying to fit in and not look conspicuous. I took communion, which I didn't know was inappropriate because I was not Catholic. No one said anything to me or seemed troubled that I did this. During the service, the nuns sang, and I was mesmerized by their beautiful voices. After the service everyone left, and I sat in the chapel by myself and continued to weep. The priest who had conducted the service had walked back into the chapel from behind me. He walked down the aisle to where I was sitting, knelt behind me, and leaned over my left shoulder. He prayed for a few minutes out loud. I never looked at the priest, but I recognized his voice from the service. After he finished praying, he left, and from behind the closed curtains the nuns sang two beautiful and moving songs. I was the only one still in the chapel, and almost hysterical now. I couldn't believe this was happening to me, and I was overcome with joy and love from God. It took a while for me to compose myself before I went to the Speak Room to meet with Sister Rosemary and Mother Anne again.

It was now about 9 am. Sister Rosemary and Mother Anne had more questions about my Godly experiences, and we talked for another two hours. After we finished talking, they told me that they would like to show me the area in the monastery that they were preparing to renovate. I was pleased that they offered to do this, but I didn't realize what an extraordinary gesture this was.

We left the Speak Room and met in the hallway. This was the first time we were not separated by a barrier. We then walked through a door behind us that Mother Anne immediately closed. Mother Anne stood in front of me and said with the deepest sincerity, "Welcome to Cloister." This struck me as odd. I wondered why she was welcoming me to my business—Cloister Car Wash. Mother Anne could see that I was perplexed. A big smile came over her face and she said, "You have no idea what I'm talking about, do you?" I admitted that I didn't. She told me that the moment I walked through the door, I had stepped into a cloistered area—an area that is restricted from outsiders. I learned later that having permission to take me into a cloistered area was very unusual and very special.

We walked down polished circular steps and along walls that were adorned by beautiful religious paintings. I was taken through areas where the nuns prepared and ate meals. I saw bedrooms, rooms that are called cells. These rooms are about 10 feet by 10 feet, with a cot for a bed, and a simple desk and chair. There was nothing hanging on the painted block walls. The cells were simple and very clean. I felt humbled being in these rooms. This was the area that needed renovation. I saw the work area where the nuns used to make communion wafers that they sold to Catholic churches. I was taken through their print shop and the room where they create greeting cards that they sell to the general public to raise money for the monastery. I also saw the area where they make rosaries. We also walked around the gated grounds where they garden, harvest, and keep bees. It still had not sunk in how privileged I was to see all this. I was so naïve that I thought this was no more special than my giving someone a tour of one of my car washes. It was very impressive, even in its simplicity, and I felt a spiritual presence as powerful as any of my Godly experiences. During the tour I learned that construction on the monastery was started in 1958 and completed in 1970. Mother Anne and Sister Martha from the current community of nuns actually helped to build the monastery. They carried stones to the stone masons, mixed mortar, and did a lot of hard labor during construction. The nuns have a website, www.heartsawake.org, which I encourage you to visit. It explains their history, lifestyle, spiritual mission, and the work they do to show their love for God, support their monastery, and serve others.

After we finished touring the various areas of the monastery, we went back to the Speak Room. I was again told that what I saw was very restricted. Priests were not allowed to go into the cloistered areas that I was taken through. By now it was clear to me how special it was that I had been shown the inner workings of the monastery. We talked more, and I recall a lot of conversation about the light I saw on the hill the night the Grace Friendship and Partnership Contract was created. We also talked about Roger. The conversation I had with Sister Rosemary and Mother Anne about Roger got me thinking about him. I had not given up that he would accept God as our business partner and that one day we would form a partnership. I got the strong feeling while I was sitting with the nuns that God wanted me to try to connect with him again. It crossed my mind that I could drive from Terre Haute to London, Ontario, Canada, to check out an area where he was thinking about building a car wash. I talked to Sister Rosemary and Mother Anne about this. They said that if I felt God was calling me to do this, I should make the trip. I decided to stay another night, visit with the nuns in the morning before I left, and then drive to Canada.

Around noon, I called Rhoda and asked her to overnight my passport to the attention of Mother Anne at the monastery. Rhoda was not happy about this, and she was getting a little more than curious about what was going on with me. I was going to be spending a part of a fourth day with the nuns, and would not be home until after I made a lengthy trip to Canada, not far from Toronto, before driving back to Lancaster County. I did my best to explain myself, and I promised Rhoda that I would make sense of all of this when I got home. Rhoda mailed my passport so I would get it the next day before I left the nuns.

It was now August 10th. I went to Mass again that morning. I was able to keep my emotions in check this time, and observe the beauty and spirituality of the service. Mother Anne had told me that all of the nuns in the monastery wanted to meet me, and that I should come to the Speak Room after Mass. When the curtains opened, Mother Ann and Sister Rosemary were sitting by themselves. We talked for a few minutes, and Mother Anne asked me if it was okay to invite the other nuns into the Speak Room. I said, "Of course," and then they filed in one by one and sat down. All of the nuns briefly introduced themselves. They were different ages and from all over the world. Some spoke perfect

English, and some spoke broken English, but it was a joy to hear from them and to learn a little bit about their backgrounds. They talked about what they did at the monastery. Some spoke about their talents and personal interests, and they were all friendly and had outgoing personalities. They were a lot of fun to be with, but there was also an overwhelming sense of their commitment to serving God.

Mother Anne asked me to tell the nuns about myself. I was exhausted, and a little tired of talking about myself, but I mustered the energy to tell them about Rhoda and my children, my business, and some things about my personal interests. I didn't go into as much detail as I had with Sister Rosemary and Mother Anne on the previous days. Mother Anne did not ask me to talk about my Godly experiences. After I spoke to the nuns, I recalled the Cloister bags that I had packed, and I said, "I have brought gifts for you." There were 12 nuns, including Sister Rosemary and Mother Anne, the exact number of bags I had packed and brought with me. The coincidence was so startling to me that I started to cry. I told the nuns that I was crying because God had given me a message to bring 12 bags, and I thought this was a Godly moment. I pulled myself together, and two of the nuns went with me to my truck to get the Cloister gift bags.

The nuns were thrilled with what I had brought them, and they asked me questions about how the items were used at the car washes. After my visit, I got a fun photograph from the monastery showing the nuns wearing Team Cloister greeter aprons. The bag I put everything in said Team Cloister, not Cloister Car Wash. That made me think about how appropriate the bag and apron were because the nuns were a cloistered team that served God. It brings a smile to my face when I think about the nuns using the Cloister window cleaner when they do housekeeping around the monastery.

I had the feeling that I was not in control of anything that was happening to me. God was in control. I had felt that way before I left on my trip, and the feeling grew stronger during my time at the monastery. Rhoda will tell you that when I called her during my visit, she sensed this. I was a different person, being guided by a spiritual force that I had no control over. This was a good thing, but it was also a little scary to both of us. Rhoda said she could hear it in my voice—a reverence, a giving of myself to God, that she had not sensed before. She said at times I sounded somewhat disoriented and overwhelmed, and emotionally in a state I had never been before, but she knew I was safe and in a good place. Rhoda had thought about converting to

Catholicism and becoming a nun when she was young, so I thought she could relate to where I was and what I was feeling. I had spent almost four full days at the most spiritually fulfilling place I had ever been. It was truly a Godly experience.

My passport had arrived, and I remember Mother Anne being excited to deliver it to me. I decided I was still going to make the 12-hour trip to Canada to check out the area where Roger planned on building a car wash. It was hard to say goodbye to Sister Rosemary and Mother Anne. I think my time at the monastery was as special for the nuns as it was for me. Sister Rosemary and Mother Anne wanted Rhoda, and someone else who knew me, to visit them without me. I planned to ask Rhoda and my assistant Alicia to make the trip as soon as possible. As I was getting ready to leave, I had a strong feeling that Sister Rosemary, Mother Anne, and the Terre Haute monastery would forever be an important part of my personal and spiritual life.

I left the monastery around noon on August 10 and arrived in London, Ontario, around 11 pm and found a place to stay. I spent a memorable four hours the next morning with a taxicab driver that you will read about in Chapter XIII Feelings. I left London around noon on August 11. I was eager to get home to Rhoda. I had a lot to tell her about my time with the nuns, and I had not spoken with her since I left Terre Haute.

When I got home around midnight, I was excited to talk to Rhoda. I woke her from a deep sleep and immediately started to tell her about the nuns. Rhoda was not very interested, and a little confused, so I decided to talk to her more about my visit the next morning.

We got up early, and I immediately started to talk about my trip. "Rhoda, you have to go there; the nuns want to meet you," I pleaded with her. I told Rhoda that it was important to me, and to the nuns, that she visit with them, but Rhoda did not want to go. I said to Rhoda, "I never ask you to do anything for me, but I am asking you now—I am begging you. Please go see the nuns." Rhoda refused to go. She had always believed my Godly experiences, but going to visit with Carmelite nuns to talk about me and these experiences was just too much for her. She told me that she thought all of this was "a little strange." She was just overwhelmed with what I told her about my visit, and she was uncomfortable with what I was asking her to do. To add to her uneasiness, I told her that Sister Rosemary and Mother Anne wanted to meet her and someone else who knew me, and they didn't want me to come with them.

I continued to plead with Rhoda all day, and she finally, but reluctantly, agreed to go. We asked my assistant, Alicia, to go with Rhoda. Alicia knew me well. She had started working at the car wash when she was 15, and had worked her way up to my assistant. We had spent many years working together. Alicia said that she would go, and because I felt there was a real urgency to do this, Rhoda and Alicia made plans to fly to Terre Haute a few days later.

Rhoda and Alicia flew to Indianapolis, Indiana, rented a car, and made the one hour drive to the monastery in Terre Haute. It wasn't long after they had arrived and spent some time with Sister Rosemary and Mother Anne that I got a phone call from Rhoda. She said excitedly, "These are the most God-loving and wonderful people I have ever met!"

Rhoda and Alicia slept in the monastery and ate with the priests. They were not permitted to eat with the nuns. They spent a lot of time talking with Sister Rosemary and Mother Anne in the Speak Room. All four of them would meet on the guest side of the room, with four chairs set up in a circle. Sister Rosemary and Mother Anne wanted to know everything Rhoda could remember about my Godly experiences. They asked a lot of questions about our business and personal life. They wanted to know about Rhoda, too—her family, her background, how she met me, her role in the business, and more. They asked Alicia a lot of questions, and she gave them input on what it was like to work closely with me. Rhoda told me the four days she was there with Alicia were unlike anything she had ever experienced. Rhoda believes the nuns thought there was something special about my Godly experiences, and the depth and intensity of their questions were designed to help the nuns draw some valid and meaningful conclusions about what I had told them. Alicia was taken with the experience of being with the nuns at the monastery as much as Rhoda was. Rhoda told me that they both felt "reformed." While they were at the monastery, Rhoda and Alicia didn't watch television or venture off the grounds. In a way, they were cloistered just like the nuns. They were totally occupied—maybe engulfed—by the experience of being there.

They got to meet and spend some time with all of the nuns. Rhoda and Alicia went to Mass each day and took communion as I had. No one said anything to them about this, just as they hadn't said anything to me. It wasn't until Rhoda attended Sister Rosemary's mother's funeral in February of 2007 that a close friend of Sister Rosemary told Rhoda that you shouldn't take communion at a Catholic

Mass unless you're Catholic. Rhoda and Alicia spent a good deal of time working on the grounds of the monastery. They both mowed the huge property, each of them using large riding mowers, but they mostly took care of the numerous flower beds and vegetable gardens. Rhoda has a knack for flowers. She started the flower planting at our first two car washes, and her work set the tone for how the grounds of our car washes looked until we sold the business in 2012. Rhoda and Alicia made the grounds of the monastery look even more beautiful than they had looked before their visit. Rhoda said her time with the nuns was one of the most wonderful experiences of her life. They flew back home on August 18th. To say I was excited to sit down with Rhoda and Alicia to hear about their trip would be an understatement.

Rhoda fell in love with the nuns, and they fell in love with her. She developed a very close relationship with Sister Rosemary, as I did. Rhoda sat with Sister Rosemary at the luncheon that followed her mother's funeral. Sister Rosemary gave Rhoda a ring that she had received when she first became a teaching nun. When she became a Carmelite nun, she was not allowed to wear the ring, and she gave it to her mother. Her mother wore the ring until her death.

Rhoda will have a deep connection to the nuns for the rest of her life. She has been back to the monastery several times, including a trip with Bob Ruhe, my co-writer, which they made to do research prior to our starting work on this book. I felt it was important that Bob meet the nuns and experience firsthand the spirituality of the monastery. I didn't go because I was in New Zealand.

In October of 2005, two months after Rhoda and Alicia visited with the nuns, I found out that due to the severe allergies of some of the nuns, they needed to install air-conditioning in the dormitory area. This was part of the renovations they had told me about. The grounds at the monastery also needed attention. I offered to send a crew to help. Randy, his wife Arlene, along with their four children, and I made the trip. We were joined by Wayne, who did artwork and signage for the car washes, and Luanne, who took care of the flowers and landscaping at Cloister. Rhoda did not make the trip because of commitments she had at home and at work. We got tools and equipment together, loaded them in two pickup trucks and a tag along trailer, and the nine of us drove to Terre Haute.

Soon after we arrived, the men got to work with Danny, the monastery's maintenance man, knocking holes in the block walls to provide openings for the ductwork for the air-conditioning. The women started working on the property, and the children helped wherever they could. I was not feeling well. This was when I started to get seriously ill, but I planned to help with the heavy work as much as possible. I had shared very little about my illness with Sister Rosemary and Mother Anne prior to this trip, but by now I was getting worse, and I told the nuns that my doctors suspected that I had Lyme disease from a tick bite. I tried to be of help to the men doing the work. I was so weak that I fell off five-foot-high scaffolding and landed on my head and shoulder while we were knocking holes in the walls in the nuns' cells to install the air-conditioning ductwork. I wasn't able to do much work after that hard fall.

Because I wasn't able to help with the maintenance work, Sister Rosemary and Mother Anne thought it would be a good time for me to meet with two priests who were at the monastery. The nuns thought it was important for me to share my Godly experiences with them. One was a visiting priest, and the other was the priest who conducted the Masses that I had attended and who kneeled behind me in the aisle and prayed. I met with the priests individually in a guest house on the monastery's property. I shared in detail with both of them the writing of the Grace contract. I also shared a few of my other experiences. Unlike with the nuns, I was doing all the talking. When I was with the nuns, I felt like a student; now I felt like a teacher because I was talking without being interrupted, and I felt very confident sharing my experiences with the priests. I mentioned before that I don't like to preach, but with the two priests I felt like a preacher. They didn't ask me any questions. I recall the visiting priest, the older of the two, having a quizzical look on his face that made me feel he was thinking about and questioning what I was saying to him. He didn't acknowledge or comment on anything I said. He just listened intently. My meeting with him lasted an hour and a half. The other priest, the one who conducted the Mass, spoke broken English that made it difficult for me to understand him when he spoke to me, but we worked through that. He was more engaged than the first priest, and he made reassuring comments about the Godly experiences I shared with him. I also spoke to him for about an hour and a half.

Randy, Wayne, and the maintenance people from the monastery worked long days while we were there. Our time to work at the monastery was limited because we were in the middle of building the Reading car wash, and we had to get back to the construction project within a few days. Randy and Wayne often said to me that they were surprised I had asked them to go on this trip because of their responsibilities in Reading. The project was under a tight deadline, and we needed the car wash to start generating income. The timing wasn't the best, but I never regretted taking them from work to help the nuns.

When we weren't working, we spent time with the nuns. The nuns loved the children, and the children loved them. One evening they played a game called Spoons, that combined playing cards and grabbing spoons. There was always one fewer spoon than there were players. The players would rapidly pass cards to their left until someone had four of a kind. That would trigger everyone grabbing for a spoon. The person who didn't get a spoon was eliminated from the game. It was a lot of fun and very rewarding to me to watch the nuns, particularly Mother Anne with all her responsibilities, play with the children.

When the work was done, everyone relaxed and spent time in the unrestricted areas of the monastery before starting our long drive back to Pennsylvania. Everyone attended a Mass. Randy told me before we left that once he slowed down, he realized what a special place the monastery was and how he felt filled with the nun's love. He said everyone was "washed in love from all the nuns." Arlene said she noticed how kind the nuns were to the children, even when they wandered into restricted areas. Before we left, the nuns gave me a painting to give to Roger. They thought the gesture would encourage him to sign the Grace contract. The next time I saw him I presented the painting to him. He took it with him, but he later told me that he gave it away, which shocked me and broke my heart. The trip was a lot of hard work, but everyone enjoyed the experience and will remember it for the rest of their lives.

It was after my first visit to the monastery in August that my relationship with Sister Rosemary and Mother Anne started to grow and become special to me. The visit in October to work at the monastery made this bond stronger. This was particularly true with Sister Rosemary.

Sister Rosemary became a Sister of St. Agnes in 1964. She was a school teacher. She became a Carmelite nun in 1976. The frequent correspondence between Sister Rosemary and me started immediately after Rhoda and Alicia visited with the nuns in August of 2005. There were phone calls, e-mails, and letters. I never replied to any of her written correspondence because writing was so hard for me because of my dyslexia. We would discuss anything she had written about when we talked on the phone. Our conversations ranged from friendly questions about my health, family, and business, to deep discussions about spirituality and my Godly experiences.

Sister Rosemary continued to call and write me after I got deathly sick near the end of 2005, but I was too ill to respond. Other than with Rhoda, I wasn't taking phone calls or keeping in touch with anyone. Sister Rosemary did stay in constant touch with Rhoda to see how I was doing. I did enjoy Sister Rosemary's letters and e-mails. They helped to lift my spirits. After my ECT treatments for depression (electroconvulsive therapy where an electroshock triggers a seizure to reset brain function), I felt physically and mentally ready to re-engage with the world, and I started to take Sister Rosemary's calls again. What was amazing to me about our friendship was the range of issues and challenges she helped me work through. When I got well enough to get back to work to complete the Reading project, I found that I had serious financial and personnel matters to deal with. Sister Rosemary was astonishingly skilled in helping me think through what I had to do. She had lived as a cloistered nun for 37 years, yet she was very savvy to the ways of the outside world. I believe God's love gave her this wisdom. She became a consultant for me, providing the type of insight you would expect to get from a seasoned business executive. If God had not called her to be a nun, she would have been a successful and very honest businessperson. It was easy to see why she was selected as the bookkeeper for the monastery.

All the nuns were surprisingly in touch with events in the world, and they constantly prayed about events occurring outside of the monastery. They give their lives to helping others through God, and at the same time they stay informed about the challenges of living in the secular world. They do this by reading and talking to visitors at the monastery, but their insight goes deeper than that. They have an emotional intelligence—an intuition— that is enviable. It's as if they have a window into our spiritual lives and our everyday challenges, and they are able to shine the light of wisdom on both.

Sister Rosemary was my spiritual mentor much more so than the minister at my church. I was not well-informed on Christian theology and the history of Christianity, and Sister Rosemary was always willing to spend time with me to talk about God and the teachings of the Bible. We spoke a lot about religion, and we often had a different point of view about religious philosophy and teachings. I would often challenge Sister Rosemary about religious beliefs, but she never got upset or combative with me about what I thought. More than anyone else, she made me comfortable talking about my religious beliefs.

One of the many talents Sister Rosemary had was playing the guitar. She told me that she loved to play, but the opportunity never came up where she played for me. She did play for Rhoda and Alicia when they visited while they had lunch with a priest. I have a photo of her playing the guitar, and you can see her love for music when you look at it. Sharing these types of personal interests was indicative of the friendship and strong bond that had developed between us.

A few years after I met Sister Rosemary, and not long after I recovered from my illness, her health started to fail. This coincided with the death of her mother, which was very hard on her. Sister Rosemary was a small person and physically frail, but she was strong in her heart. She hid her deteriorating condition for a number of years, but the last few years of her life were very difficult for her, and it became impossible to hide her sickness from others.

Mother Anne shared with me that Sister Rosemary suffered from dermatomyositis, a disease that attacks the skin and muscles. This can lead to problems swallowing and eventually malnutrition. She also suffered from Addison's disease, which can cause dizziness and fainting. I was taken by how both Sister Rosemary and I suffered through serious illnesses. I felt during my time of illness and depression that I was "being poured out," and close to being called to God's kingdom. I think Sister Rosemary felt the same during the years that she was sick. Just like me, she had difficulty walking and functioning on a daily basis. She reached a point where she would wear a helmet because she was so prone to falling and hitting her head. She could hardly get out of bed. She had to be taken care of by the other nuns, just as Rhoda had taken care of me. I could also see the deterioration in her handwriting. She sometimes typed her letters, but most of them were handwritten, and her handwriting was beautiful. Even with my difficulty reading, they were easy and fun to read. The deterioration in her handwriting eventually reached a point where I could no longer read her letters. Her last few years were painful, but she had incredible faith and a tremendous love for God, and she knew at the end of her journey that she would be rewarded with

God's glory. Sister Rosemary showed me that faith in God makes death so much easier to accept. This is a lesson for all of us.

Sister Rosemary only ever asked one thing of me. That was to join the Catholic Church, which I have not done. I have thought about this, and I plan to visit the Catholic Church in Wanaka, New Zealand to talk to a priest about conversion. I will give the priest a copy of this book. I would consider becoming a Catholic to honor Sister Rosemary.

Sister Rosemary died on June 2, 2013. She was 69 years old. I had very little contact with her during the last few months of her life because she was so ill, but Rhoda and I were blessed to know her for eight years. Rhoda and I went to the services at the monastery, and I estimate they were attended by 125 people. The casket was displayed at the altar of the chapel that was filled with loved ones. We walked up to the casket with Mother Anne at our side and stood crying as we looked at Sister Rosemary's body. After the service, we walked to a cemetery on the monastery's property where many other nuns were buried. After Sister Rosemary's burial, Mother Anne asked Rhoda and me if we wanted to see Sister Rosemary's cell in the cloistered area before we left. We said we did, and we walked with Mother Anne to Sister Rosemary's room. I had not seen this room before. She was moved to this room when her health started to fail so that she would be more comfortable. The room was bigger than her other room, and it had a bathroom and a window, but I was still taken by how simple it was. The simplicity made the room feel "pure" to me. There was a small cot pressed against the wall. There was a small desk with a chair. There were very few personal items. The aura of the room was spiritual, and its simplicity and cleanliness made it very beautiful. Mother Anne opened Sister Rosemary's desk drawer. There were very few items in it. There was no clutter like you would usually see in someone's desk. Mother Anne took a ballpoint pen from the desk and said to me, "This pen was very special to Sister Rosemary. I know she would want you to have it." I know that Sister Rosemary wrote me many letters with that pen, and I will always cherish the thought of her wanting me to have it.

I had a very special friendship with Sister Rosemary. She is one of the most influential people in my life. This friendship was based on my incredible respect for her and my appreciation for the spiritual guidance that she gave me. I respected her for her sacrifices and for her love for God. I am thankful for her sincere interest in my well-being, my family, and my business. I also give thanks for her desire to help me to understand my Godly experiences and for her encouragement to continue my journey with God. Sister Rosemary was so filled with compassion and love that she believed that the pain of her sickness was to lessen the pain that others felt when they were sick or troubled. I know that she anguished over my suffering when I was sick. Mother Anne told me that Sister Rosemary would not allow her suffering to be wasted. She gave her suffering to God for whoever needed it, and that included me. The Bible teaches us that we are often tested, sometimes after good things happen to us and sometimes after a good life is lived. I mentioned earlier in this book that Randy taught me this is called a Refiner's Fire. An illness like Sister Rosemary and I fought our way through is that sort of test. I know that it strengthened her to receive God's eternal love and she is now with God in Heaven.

I was introduced to the Carmelite nuns through Sister Rosemary. All my initial communication was with Sister Rosemary, and my first visit to the monastery centered on Sister Rosemary. If Sister Rosemary had not believed the Godly experiences that I shared with her, I don't believe she would have asked me to share them with Mother Anne. That is what brought Mother Anne into my life, and I am very thankful for that.

I grew close to Mother Anne after Sister Rosemary passed away. I don't talk to her as much as I did with Sister Rosemary, and Mother Anne does not initiate conversation like Sister Rosemary did. Mother Anne and I talk on the phone several times a year. I can talk to her as openly and honestly as I did with Sister Rosemary. Mother Anne is one of my spiritual counselors, and I listen to her. She does not preach to me. She has a warm and kind voice that makes it easy to respond to her suggestions. She gave me feedback on how she interpreted my experiences that was very meaningful to me. She told me that my experiences were not common; there are not many people who have left a record and written about them or made them public. It seems that those who have described their Godly experiences have done so because their spiritual director wanted to evaluate what has happened in their life, or they were inspired to write about the events to motivate others to be aware of God in their lives. The second reason was part of my motivation. Mother Anne told me it can be very confusing and frightening to have these experiences without the guidance of others who understand the works of God. I appreciate the guidance that Sister Rosemary and Mother Anne gave me. Mother Anne said that God often chooses individuals who may see themselves as inadequate, perhaps illiterate. Was I chosen because I am dyslexic? I think it's a miracle that I wrote a book. God also chooses those who are unworthy, such as someone who is living a sinful life, like St. Paul, who was persecuting Christians. She said that God often uses the "little ones" to accomplish God's works as they put fewer obstacles in the way. Some have had extraordinary Godly experiences and then failed God by choosing their own desires which were contrary to God's grace. Only later did they respond to God in a way that was worthy of the gift they had received. She concluded, "If the experience is from God, it will bear fruit for others. The individual is only an instrument that God uses." This book is an instrument that I hope will bear fruit for others.

God is first in Mother Anne's life, but she is also knowledgeable and street-smart. She stays in touch with events outside the monastery. I have been impressed with her understanding of "fair play" in business and in life. Solutions to conflicts and problems we deal with are rarely black and white, and Mother Anne, as well as Sister Rosemary, always helped me to navigate the gray areas that we live with every day.

Mother Anne is still the leader of the monastery. A nun is elected by the other nuns to serve as the Prioress. She can serve for two consecutive terms before she has to step down. Then, she can be re-elected after one full term has passed. Mother Anne has been re-elected by the other nuns because of her leadership qualities. She is thorough, warm-hearted, smart, and a natural leader. Even in a monastery there are arguments and disagreements, and Mother Anne is the one who sorts these conflicts out and keeps everyone working together. She is a magnificent sister of God.

I believe that the phone call from Bill Barclay that led me to send a donation to the Carmelite nuns was a gift from God. The spiritual force that made me visit them and gave me the energy to talk Rhoda into visiting them was Godly. Taking 12 gift bags on my first trip to the monastery was a Godly moment. Spending four days with Sister Rosemary and Mother Anne was a Godly experience that deepened my spirituality. Rhoda's love and help was the most important factor in getting me through my illness in 2005 and 2006, but I believe the nuns' prayers for me during that time were a Godly experience because their prayers helped to save my life. Sister Rosemary's presence in my life during that time of darkness was Godly, because it helped to strengthen my faith during a difficult time. My relationship with the nuns, which continues to this day, is another example of God's grace.

I have never met people closer to God than the cloistered Carmelite nuns. They are special people, spiritually beyond other devout people I have met or known.

They gave God a voice for me, and an understanding of God's grace.

View of Rhoda and Mike's farm in Lancaster County, Pennsylvania, that they sold in 2011. This is the path that God's light/glow traveled the night Mike created the Grace Contract. The light twice moved toward Mike from wide to narrow at the speed of someone walking. Mike was standing at the spot where the light comes to a point.

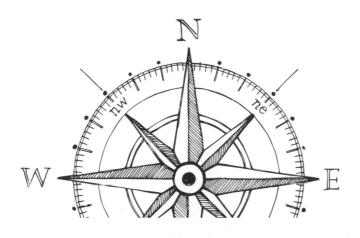

XIII.

Feelings

In the last chapter, I wrote about how my close friend, Bill Barclay, had mentioned that I never preached to him, and that I had never brought up God's name to him, but that he always knew I had a special relationship with God. He said that he could feel this when he was in my presence. This was the first of four times when someone told me that they sensed my relationship with God. Perhaps other people sensed it too but didn't tell me.

This chapter is about a surveyor, a taxi driver, and a medical technician: three strangers who told me they sensed something Godly, which opened up discussion about my experiences. These discussions occurred without my saying anything about spirituality or God. The surveyor and the taxi driver told me that they knew something Godly had happened to me. The medical technician, without any prompting, just started to talk about God, and that conversation led to an extraordinary gesture on her part. I believe that these people had a special relationship with God—that they were believers. I believe that you must have faith to feel God's presence. I believe it was God's plan for us to meet and have these discussions.

The Surveyor

My experience with the surveyor occurred a month after creating the Grace Friendship and Partnership Contract. I had decided to install a wooden fence at my farm in Lancaster County. The fence was to be installed on the property's borderline, from the bottom to the top of the hill, close to where I had the Godly experience the night the Grace contract was created. I wanted the fence to be just inside the edge of my property. I also wanted to make sure that the large rock I sat on to pray was entirely on my property. The rock, six feet in diameter and two feet high, had been moved by a bulldozer from a spot nearby to give me the best view of my farm. I was concerned that a part of it was on my neighbor's land. Surveying work had to be done to locate precisely where my property line was. I was also thinking about asking the surveyor if he could mark on my property deed the exact spot where I was standing when I saw the Godly light.

I hired Ron Hershey to do the surveying work. Ron had done some work for me over the years, but we didn't know each other well. We certainly had never talked about religion or spirituality. On the day that Ron was surveying, I drove to my farm to see how he was coming along with laying out the fence line. I found him at the top of the hill, close to where my experience had occurred. We said hello to each other, and then we talked a little about the surveying work he was close to completing.

I had driven a steel bar into the ground at the spot where I had experienced the Godly light. I spoke with Ron to confirm that he could mark that exact spot on the deed, but I didn't tell him why I wanted to do that. He said that he could, so I walked Ron a short distance down the hill to show him where I had placed the steel bar. I wanted to make sure that anybody could locate this exact spot forever, even if the property line changed, or if the land was sold off and developed. The spot was sacred to me, and I wanted it to be identified for all time. Ron didn't express any curiosity about what I was asking him to do. He didn't ask me any questions, and I didn't offer an explanation. Ron said, "No problem," and he told me that he would make sure the exact spot was marked on the deed.

Ron and I chatted for a few more minutes, and then I started to walk away to head back to work. I had walked maybe 30 feet when Ron yelled out to me, "Something Godly happened at this spot, didn't it?" His remark caught me off guard, and my emotions got the better of me. When I regained my composure, I put a big smile on my face and turned back to Ron and said, "Yes, it did. Yes, it did, Ron." Our eyes locked for a few seconds, then we nodded knowingly at each other, and I slowly walked away.

I believe that this moment with Ron was a Godly experience for both of us. I believe God's presence was still on the hill, a month after the Grace Friendship and Partnership Contract was created. I always felt that God's presence was inside of me, and maybe that presence was stronger during this time. Ron either felt God's presence on the hill, or sensed it radiating from inside of me. Maybe he sensed both. I always wondered if other people could sense God's presence when they were around me. I often had the feeling that they could, even though they never told me that. I don't mean to imply that there was a spiritual aura around me, but

I do think that some people could sense that Godly things had happened to me. Ron specifically said that he sensed it, even though we weren't talking about my experiences. I spoke to Ron recently, and we talked about our time on the hill. That was 12 years ago, and he remembered it as if it happened yesterday. Ron reconfirmed that he strongly sensed that something Godly had occurred at the spot that I wanted marked on the deed.

The location of the rock that I sat on to pray was just as important to me as the spot where I saw the Godly light. The fence was installed just inside my property line, but the rock was never moved from the place it was the night of my experience. Ron confirmed that half of the rock was on my property, and half was on my neighbor's land. The fence was installed over the rock, and my neighbor never said a word about it because it was at a remote part of their property. Ron marked the exact spot where I saw the light, and he put this on the deed. I placed an antique millstone grinding wheel, four feet in diameter and approximately 10 inches thick, at that spot to clearly identify the location.

If you look at the aerial view of my farm from Google Earth, you can see the hill where I had my Godly experience. The round millstone grinding wheel near the top of the hill, just before the tree line, identifies the spot where I was standing when I saw the Godly light. Rhoda and I sold the property that we called Grace Farm to a couple from Massachusetts on December 30, 2011. I told the new owners about my Godly experience at the farm. The husband and wife are both medical doctors, and they are devoutly spiritual people. Rhoda and I have a warm invitation to visit them anytime. They recently bought the neighboring farm, so now the rock is entirely on their beautiful property.

The Taxi Driver

My experience with the taxi driver occurred in August of 2005. I had driven to Terre Haute, Indiana, to visit the Carmelite nuns, when I recalled Roger from Canada telling me about a city in Ontario where he was thinking about building his circular-design car wash. After my visit with the nuns, I made the 12-hour drive to the town of London in Ontario, Canada, to check out the area. I was curious about what Roger was planning, but I was also drawn to go there by something stronger than just curiosity. I had the sense that God wanted me to do this. I planned to drive back to Lancaster County after I looked around the London area.

When I arrived in London, a city with a population

of more than 300,000 people, I called a taxicab company and asked them to send a driver to the convenience store where I had stopped to get gas. His name was Ataur. I wanted Ataur to show me around the town and the surrounding suburbs. I wanted to see the types of homes in the area, retail businesses, major roads and the amount of car traffic, and the busiest parts of the town. I wanted to see if Roger had picked an area that I thought could support a car wash. I also felt that a taxi driver could offer me some unique insights about the community, and give me some feedback on the reputation of the other car washes in London.

Ataur was a young man, probably about 30 years old, and very friendly. He was dark-skinned, and I thought he might be from India. I told him that I would need his services for a few hours, and I told him why I was there and what I wanted to accomplish. We immediately hit it off, and conversation came very easily. After we drove around for 30 minutes or so, he said, "Your trip has something to do with God, doesn't it?" I was as surprised at his remark as I was when Ron Hershey, the surveyor, had made a similar comment. I replied, "Yes, it does. My trip here was prompted by a Godly experience that I had because of meeting a Canadian businessman." Ataur told me that he could sense a spiritual presence in me, and I wondered if God's presence was still radiating from me many months after my experience the night the Grace contract was created. I also thought my time with the Carmelite nuns might be giving me a spiritual glow. Whatever it was, Ataur told me he could sense a Godly presence, just as Ron Hershey had sensed it, even though I had not said a word to him about my experiences.

I told Ataur about meeting Roger and Tom. I told him about the experience on the hill and how I saw the Godly light. I told him about my recent visit to the Carmelite nuns and the talks I had with them about my experiences. He was so taken by what I was telling him that he pulled over, stopped the car, and turned off the meter. He asked me if he could take me to meet his parents at their home. I told him I would be honored to meet them.

Before we went to meet his parents, we finished our drive around the London area. I saw a number of suitable locations to build a car wash, and I quickly determined that the London area was a good choice for the type of car wash that Roger was planning.

The home of Ataur's parents was beautiful and much larger than I expected. His parents greeted us in the foyer. I remember that they were wearing sandals but were dressed in typical Western attire. They were dark-skinned like their son, and I was sure they were from India. It was not clear to me if they were of the Hindu or Christian faith. They spoke English, but we didn't have a lot of conversation. I could sense how excited they were that their son had brought me to meet them. I got the impression that it was very unusual for him to do this. We didn't have any religious conversation, and yet, without much talking, I felt that my time with them was a spiritual experience for each of us. I believe that they sensed the same thing in me that the surveyor and the Carmelite nuns had sensed, and I believe our time together was very meaningful for them. It was certainly meaningful to me. Without a lot of conversation, we made a connection. You never know how and why God brings people together. I believe that's God's way of showing love to all of us, regardless of what faith we practice.

I spent three hours with Ataur before he took me back to my truck. When I asked what I owed him, he just smiled and would not take any money. The smile on his face was priceless. We got out of the cab, hugged each other, and said goodbye. We never talked about his background. That really wasn't important. What was important was that our lives connected, and we were spiritually affected by our time together. I believe it was a Godly experience for both of us.

During the writing of this section of the book, I tracked Ataur down from a photograph of his cab that included the cab company's phone number. We had a wonderful talk, and he told me that he remembered the time we spent together like it was yesterday.

The Medical Technician

In the winter of 2005, a few months after my experience with the taxi driver, I had become so extremely sick from my illness and depression that my doctors sent me to get an ultrasound. This was done at an outpatient care clinic near my office in Ephrata. I was greeted in the lobby by a young woman who was the technician who was going to do the procedure.

The young woman escorted me into a dark room where the equipment was located. She explained to me how the procedure worked and what I should expect, and then she had me lie on my side as she positioned herself behind me to do the ultrasound. We talked for a few minutes before she started the procedure, and I sensed in her words and her manner that there was something very special about her. She surprised me when she suddenly brought up the topic of God. I have no idea what made her think to talk to me about God, but her remarks prompted me to tell her about my Godly experience with the writing of the Grace Friendship and Partnership Contract. I told her about the experience on the hill and how I saw the Godly light, and I told her about my time with the Carmelite nuns, just as I had done with the taxi driver. We talked for a long time, and we got into a deep, spiritual conversation. I'm not sure what her religious beliefs were, but I remember thinking how we were totally in tune with each other, and how she deeply listened to what I was sharing with her. It always pleases me when people take an interest in what I have to say about my experiences. It makes me feel that I am adding something positive to their lives.

This connection felt very similar to what had happened with the surveyor and the taxi driver, and just like the other two, it did not originate from anything that I said or did. The technician seemed to sense that I was someone she could talk to about God and living a spiritual life. It was every bit as much of a Godly experience for me as it was with the surveyor and taxi driver. When the ultrasound was done, we hugged and said goodbye, and I left. No one likes to go through medical procedures, but

I remember having a very warm and special feeling about the time I spent at the clinic because of the conversation I had with the technician. I believe we connected because we shared a willingness to talk about God.

Several weeks after the ultrasound, the technician stopped by my office. I was not expecting her, but I was very pleased that she came to see me. I invited her to visit with me, and she told me about how meaningful the time we had spent together was for her. She told me how appreciative she was that I had shared my experiences with her. She had brought with her a small black satchel. She opened the bag and carefully lifted out a black rosary that she had made. The rosary was made from glass beads, hand strung on silver wire, with a silver crucifix attached. She told me that she had never made rosary beads before, but she was so inspired by our conversation that she had to do this as a gift for me. The rosary beads were stunningly beautiful, and I will cherish them for the rest of my life. I never saw her again, and I regret that I don't remember her name. The rosary beads always remind me of the brief, but memorable, time that we spent together.

The surveyor, the taxi driver, and the medical technician sensed God's presence in me. Bill Barclay told me that he sensed this in me when he told me about the Carmelite nuns and the miracle of their prayers. I believe the nuns also sensed it during my first visit with them. I don't think of myself as a disciple of God, but I do enjoy telling people about God's miracles. I guess we are all disciples of God if we share our faith with others. I do hope that I carry God's glory within me and that some other people sense this and are touched by it. All of us have the opportunity to touch others this way if we keep God first and make God the most important part of our lives.

Messages to guide us are everywhere if we open our hearts and minds to see them.

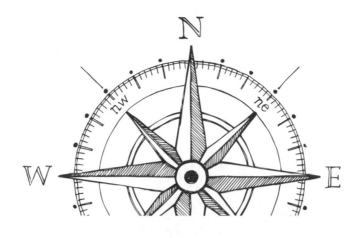

XIV.

Message

In the fall of 2015, I left New Zealand to spend a month in Lancaster County, Pennsylvania. When I make these 28-hour trips, I always look forward to catching up with old friends at breakfast or lunch.

Soon after I arrived, I got a phone call from my close friend Lowell Roth. He asked me to join him for breakfast. I hadn't seen Lowell for a few years, so I was very pleased that he had called. I have known Lowell since I was 12 years old. He is 17 years older than I and someone whom I admire and respect. We worked together for several years in the same small office at my family's business where Lowell was Purchasing Manager and I was one of three buyers. Lowell always conducted himself ethically, and with fairness and compassion for others in his business dealings. He is the type of person who always has a smile on his face and a positive outlook about everything. He is a very spiritual man and is very active in his church. His spirituality and positive attitude helped him to rebound from the death of his beautiful wife, Ruthie, in an automobile accident. Lowell has told me many times that he thinks of me as a son, and my nickname for him is "Big Daddy."

We met for breakfast at a restaurant just outside of Ephrata. Lowell and I shared a love for God, but I didn't recall ever sharing my Godly experiences with him. During breakfast we started talking about God, and I told him about a few of the experiences I have written about in this book. I had no intention of talking with Lowell about my experiences that day, but the conversation just naturally went that way, as it often does. When I get into conversations about my experiences, I am always paying attention to how the person I am sharing them with is reacting. Are they interested or turned off by what I am saying? People always want to know more, and Lowell was no exception. He was fascinated with what I was telling him, and I think a little surprised that I had never told him about my experiences before.

As you know by now, I get very emotional when I talk about my experiences. Sometimes I can keep my emotions in check. Other times, I just weep as I go through them. I didn't want to get emotional in the restaurant in front of my dear friend, but I couldn't help it. I cried uncontrollably as we spoke. Lowell kept his composure and tried to comfort me, but I'm sure it was awkward for him. I couldn't help but notice that many of the people in the restaurant were looking at us.

We spent two hours talking. I went into detail about the writing of the Grace Friendship and Partnership Contract and my experience with the Carmelite nuns. I felt emotionally drained talking with Lowell, just as I usually did when I shared my Godly experiences, and I worried about what my friend was thinking of me. I often feel "beat up" after I talk about my experiences. Sometimes I am so drained that I feel like I was in a gang fight and my gang didn't show up. That's how I felt after talking with Lowell.

When our breakfast was over, we said goodbye and hugged each other. Lowell thanked me from the bottom of his heart for sharing some of my experiences with him. Because we were such close friends, and because he was deeply spiritual, I could tell that what we had talked about had a big impact on him. I think he felt he learned something about me, and how God works through people, that day. I walked with Lowell to his car. We shook hands and promised to stay in touch with each other.

As I walked to my pickup truck, I thought about how emotionally draining my time with Lowell had been, and how embarrassed I was that people were looking at me in the restaurant. Over the past 10 years, I had shared my Godly experiences with hundreds of people. As I walked to my truck, I talked to God, and I questioned if I should continue to share my experiences. I felt beat up and exhausted again. I was starting to feel that I didn't need to share them anymore. I asked God if I had shared them enough. I asked God if my work was done. I thought about what I had said the night the Grace contract was created when I totally surrendered to God: *God, you have given me so many wonderful moments with you, not just tonight, but throughout my life. I don't need any more. I have been blessed. I've had more than my fair share of your love. Please share your grace with others.*

I got into my truck and drove about one mile toward Ephrata until I came to a traffic light. As I sat at a traffic light, I looked to my right and saw this message on the announcement board at the Bergstrasse Lutheran Church: *God gave you a message to share. Don't keep it to yourself.* This reminded me of the passage in the book *A Look at Life from a Deer Stand* that revealed to me what to do about my sons' fighting. It was the second time something like that had happened.

When I read that sign, I went to pieces. Here I was questioning if I should continue to tell people about my experiences. I was getting tired of the emotional strain of sharing them with others. I was asking God if I had done enough, and God answered me. There could not have been a clearer answer to my question, and it appeared the instant I was struggling with what I should do.

Was this just a coincidence? Maybe it was. If it was, it was a one-in-a-million coincidence. I believe in my heart it was God responding to me. Even though it was a short experience—just a moment in time—it had the same powerful impact on me as any other experience I have shared with you. God was telling me that my work was not done. God wanted me to share my experiences with as many people as possible, and I have continued to do that. That message played a role in my deciding to write this book. This book allows me to connect with people I can't personally talk to, as emotional as that is for me, and I will continue to share my experiences by speaking about them with people I meet. I also hope this book encourages readers to talk to others about Godly experiences, whether they are experiences in this book or experiences they have had personally. Talking about God will start a dialogue that will change people's lives.

There is no doubt in my mind that the message I saw in front of the church was a Godly experience. It was a message from God.

God is the most important part of my life. God is at the very top of my love box. I believe I will continue to have experiences. They will occur because I have strong faith, and my heart and mind are open to them. I am prepared to receive them, and I will share them for as long as God wants me to do that.

If you have faith, and open your heart and your mind to God's love, you will find God's messages all around you.

These messages are God's grace.

Mike with his friends from Germany and Israel who took an interest in this book and the Tarras Church while working at Grace Farm New Zealand in 2018

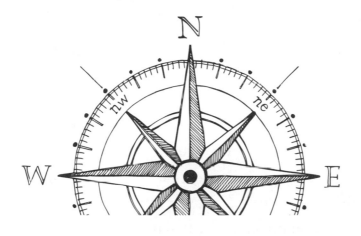

XV.

Never-Ending Grace

I first learned about the Tarras Church while attending Saint Columba's Church in my hometown of Wanaka. The Reverend Damon Plimmer was the vicar at Saint Columba's. I liked Damon and enjoyed his sermons. One Sunday after church, I mentioned this to a retired judge named Fred. He suggested that I attend a service at the Tarras Church, where Damon preached on the second Sunday of each month. This is the only Sunday of the month that the Tarras Church has a service. The church is 19 miles, or 30 kilometers, from where I now live in Wanaka. I was immediately drawn to the beauty and simplicity of the Tarras Church and the four-acre property that surrounds it, and I started to attend Sunday services when I could.

I found out early in 2017 that the current owners of the Tarras Church wanted to sell the property, but the Tarras community was very keen to retain the Tarras Church as a place of Christian worship. I had developed a special feeling for the church, and I wanted to help in any way that I could. One morning while I was taking a shower thinking about family, friends, and nothing else in particular, God revealed to me to "buy the church." I later came to understand that this did not mean to "own" the church.

This message is my most recent Godly experience. There were a number of events that had to come together at exactly the right time and in the right sequence to put me in a position to help the Tarras Church financially. I am humble about these events and the magnitude of my good fortune, and in no way do I want to appear boastful. This sequence of events started when Rhoda and I first visited New Zealand.

Discovering New Zealand

Our first trip was in September of 2006. This time of year is spring in New Zealand. The country had a population of 4.6 million people in 2015. Without exception, I have found the "Kiwis" to be friendly, caring, trustworthy, hardworking, and adventurous people. Kiwi is the nickname used internationally for people from New Zealand, as well as being a relatively common self-reference. The name derives from the Kiwi, a native flightless bird, which is the national symbol of New Zealand.

We flew into Auckland, which is located on the country's North Island. The North Island has three times the number of people as the South Island. Auckland is the country's largest city, with a population of 1.5 million people. The capital city of Wellington, with a population of approximately 400,000 people, is located on the North Island. The North Island is rich in Maori culture, the indigenous people of New Zealand. It is warmer than the South Island and known for its beaches, geothermal activity, and world-class scuba diving.

The north and south islands are separated by the Cook Strait, which connects the Tasman Sea to the west with the South Pacific Ocean to the east. It is a 3½-hour ferry ride to travel from Wellington, on the southern tip of the North Island, to Picton, on the northern tip of the South Island.

The South Island is known for its dramatic snowcapped-mountain scenery, glaciers, wildlife, numerous national parks, and agriculture. Christchurch, with a population of approximately 350,000 people, is the largest city on the South

Island and the third-largest city in New Zealand. In recent years, this beautiful, historic city has suffered a great deal of destruction from a number of earthquakes. Queenstown, on the South Island, is considered the adventure capital of New Zealand.

The North Island is beautiful, but the South Island is stunningly so. When Rhoda and I first visited, we started our 30-day trip by touring the North Island. I was constantly telling people how beautiful I thought New Zealand was. Almost everyone said, "If you think it's beautiful here, wait until you see the South Island." Once Rhoda and I spent time on the South Island, I was hooked. I knew I wanted to live there one day. I remember saying to Rhoda, "I am in serious trouble here!" I was just that taken by what I was seeing. Rhoda looked at me and said with an insight only she would have, "I know you are."

New Zealand is where I was called to be. It felt like home the minute I first set foot on the beautiful landscape. Rhoda could tell how taken I was with the country, and she told me on our first trip that she knew New Zealand would be a part of our future life.

Over the next six years, I went back to New Zealand at least 10 times. I made many of these trips by myself because Rhoda had obligations at home or at the business. She was the head field hockey coach at our local high school. She loved the sport and was very committed to the girls, and wouldn't travel to New Zealand during field hockey season. During these years I would tour the South Island looking for a place to live, and I made it a point to visit churches. I found the churches to be beautiful and inviting. The majority of them were small, seating 80 to 100 people. I did visit a few that were larger that seated hundreds of people. I would walk church properties and go inside when the churches weren't locked. I loved to sit in the pews and think and absorb the feeling of awe that I was getting from being there. I would often have a discussion with God, and then I would say a prayer before I left.

A locked church always bothered me. I realized that there might be good reasons to lock the church doors, but I always believed that there had to be other options. I thought about what I would do if I was ever involved with the operations of a church. I thought about the people who built these churches— the love they must have had for God. I thought about the purpose of these churches and why people were pulling away from the church. When I was able to attend a Sunday service, the attendance was usually very few and mostly elderly. I always felt that something was missing. I was concerned about the absence of middle-aged and younger people, and I wondered what I could do to change that.

I wanted to live in New Zealand. I knew I would be very happy there and that I would have an active and meaningful spiritual life. However, moving there would not be possible without selling my business. I would need the money from the sale of my company to move to New Zealand. That was just a financial reality. Plus, I wanted to become a resident and eventually a citizen, and that would require my spending extensive time in the country away from the management of my company. I knew that would not work. I had casually thought about selling my company, but I was not actively pursuing it. I soon found out that God had other plans for me.

Selling My Business

I owned and operated Cloister Car Wash (www. cloistercarwash.org) for 28 years. In 2012, I was starting to feel tired and had lost the "fire in my belly." My enthusiasm to continue to grow the business had waned. I started to think more seriously about selling the company. I also recognized that the business had grown to a size where a larger operator with an experienced management team could manage the continued growth of the company better than

I could. I wanted my 400 employees to have opportunities to grow in their careers. My entrepreneurial skills had built the business, but I started to think that maybe those skills were not the best thing for the company and the employees in the future. I had fallen in love with New Zealand, and I knew that I wanted to move there someday, but I had no date set in my mind. I knew there was no way I could move on a permanent basis without selling the business.

When I did think about selling Cloister, I kept coming back to something that always concerned me—the value of the business. I always wondered if I would ever be able to find a buyer for my business who would be willing to pay a price at which I was willing to sell. I was told the value of the business was a lot less than what I thought it should be. I admit I did not have the financial expertise to value a business. My feelings about the value of the company were based on a "gut" feeling, or my ideas about what I thought I would pay if I was buying the company. This gut feeling had driven the business forward for 28 years and had always served me well. I had learned to trust my gut, and more often than not, my instincts were correct. Some might call this "seat of the pants" management, but it worked for me. My "gut" was very much at odds with what my financial team was telling me about the value of the business. This was discouraging to me, and it kept me from actively looking for a buyer.

In the spring of 2012, I attended a car wash convention in Las Vegas where I saw Ron Peterson, a business acquaintance of 20 years, standing in the lobby. Ron and I made the usual small talk, and I told him I was feeling worn out and thinking about selling my business. Ron asked me if he could come to Pennsylvania to look at my four car washes. Ron was the main principal for Mister Car Wash. They were actively acquiring car washes around the country and were looking to buy some washes in the northeastern part of the United States where Cloister Car Wash was located. Ron mentioned that he had heard many good things about Cloister, and I had heard the same about Mister Car Wash. I told him we would arrange a visit when I got back to Lancaster County. Within weeks of our chance meeting in Las Vegas, Ron called me and we scheduled a time for him to visit. He ended up spending four days with me touring our facilities and talking with me and my managers. At the end of his visit, we sat down and Ron told me what he thought the value of my company was. It was amazing, if not a miracle, that Ron's thinking and my thinking were almost identical. Ron came up with his estimate of value without looking at our financial statements. He had been buying car washes for years, and he was so experienced with the car wash business that he could estimate the value of a company based on interviews, observations, and the volume of cars that were being washed, before taking a close look at the financial statements. He trusted his "gut feeling" just like I did. If nothing surprised him with our statements, he was confident his valuation would be accurate. Ron asked me to send him audited financial statements, and he promised to get back to me with a definitive offer, or what the next steps would be, as soon as possible. A few weeks after Ron's visit, he sent a crew of seven people who looked closely at our facilities, observed customer activity, and met with me and my management and financial teams. After they were there for several days, they went back to their office in Arizona to put together a formal offer to purchase the business. A few days later, I received a phone call from their chief financial officer, and he offered a price that was very close to what I was looking for. After some additional negotiation, we agreed on a price and moved forward with the sale of Cloister Car Wash to Mister Car Wash.

This was an exciting and yet very difficult time for me. The business was like a child to me, and I felt an obligation to the employees. My son Elton—

a very capable, loyal, and outstanding employee—worked there. I wanted the best for him, and I was concerned about his future if I sold the business. I did realize that the business had reached a point where an organization like Mister Car Wash was better equipped to grow the company more quickly, and more profitably, than I could. I believed in my heart that I was doing the right thing by selling. I still feel that way today, even though I occasionally second-guess myself. Selling my company provided the financial resources and the freedom that allowed me to move to New Zealand.

We set December 14, 2012, as the date for settlement. We wanted to finalize the sale of the business in 2012. Everything went smoothly and quickly. Mister Car Wash was the perfect company to buy the business. Ron Peterson came to my house to discuss the sale with me. He told me it was going to be the toughest thing I had ever done in my life. I didn't believe him at first. *How could that be possible?* I thought to myself. I would be out from under the pressure of running the business, and I would be able to spend more time in New Zealand, but Ron turned out to be 100 percent right. Selling something I had spent 28 years building into a successful business was very emotional and a difficult transition for me to make. The love I had for the employees, the business, and the car wash industry would be impossible to replace. It's still hard for me to drive past one of the four facilities when I am back in Pennsylvania. I'll notice changes, even small changes, and they bother me even though they may be for the best. For example, I had a very strict dress code that included red Cloister T-shirts. The managers wore white dress shirts and red ties, and now I see a variety of shirts in different colors and styles. I know Mister Car Wash didn't get to where they are without being smart operators, but it was still hard on me to see them change things I was passionate about. I also miss the contact with the people—employees, vendors, and customers. Most of the people I knew came from a connection to Cloister. The company was my whole life. This was tough to give up and get used to, and I still feel that way. When I sold the business, almost everything I knew went with it. Customers would see me around town and tell me the company wasn't the same without me. They didn't mean something was wrong; it just meant something was different— something had changed—Mike wasn't there. I was a 28-year fixture at Cloister, and to the community, Mike Mountz and Cloister Car Wash were one and the same. I take comfort in knowing that opportunities have occurred for many of the employees. Despite the hurt that came from selling, I know I did the right thing for my family, my employees, and me.

A Serious Health Scare

Rhoda's birthday is December 31st. Early that morning, a little more than two weeks after we finalized the sale of our business, she came down to the basement rec room at our home in Ephrata with a huge sticky bun that was dripping with butter. I said to her, "You're not going to eat all of that, are you?" We started laughing and she replied, "Yep, it's my birthday, and I'm going to eat the whole thing!" Rhoda said she wanted to visit her dad, who was in the hospital, and we agreed to do that after I picked up some things at the office that I still had at the Ephrata car wash where corporate headquarters was located. I was at the office a short time and was heading home when I got a text from Rhoda that said, "I need you." I had never received a message like that from her. I raced the three miles to our home and found Rhoda sitting on the sofa clutching her chest. I immediately thought that she was having a heart attack. I quickly decided that driving her to the hospital in town would be faster than waiting for an ambulance. The hospital was only five minutes from our home. I helped her into my pickup truck, and we started to drive to the Ephrata hospital. Rhoda decided that she wanted to go to the Lancaster hospital, 20 minutes farther away, because the Ephrata hospital didn't have a top-notch cardiology department. This concerned Rhoda, so she insisted that we go to Lancaster.

As we started to drive to Lancaster, Rhoda yelled, "I'm not going to make it; I'm not going to make it!" I turned around and headed to the emergency room at the Ephrata hospital. Rhoda was taken inside in a wheelchair, put on a stretcher, and connected to a number of monitors to check her vital signs. The emergency room was packed, and there was no room available for her, so they moved her stretcher into the hallway and set up a portable curtain to give her some privacy. She was in excruciating pain and was having trouble breathing, but we were told by nurses that she did not have a heart attack. I thought it had to be a heart attack, but what did I know? The nurses are the professionals. We waited for 30 minutes as Rhoda continued to suffer with extreme pain in her chest, and we still had not seen a doctor. I went to the nurses' station and insisted that Rhoda desperately needed help. A few minutes later, nurses stopped by and checked on her as best they could. Rhoda was throwing up, and I just knew that she had a heart attack. She was fine one minute in the basement of our house and in terrible pain the next minute, so I thought it couldn't be something like the flu or pneumonia. Another 20 minutes passed, and I went back to the nurses' station and got very assertive with them. I said, "Either a doctor is here in five minutes or you get an ambulance to take her to the Lancaster hospital—one or the other!"

When I got back to Rhoda, I was shaking. I was so upset and fearful. I did not like that I raised my voice and made demands, but I felt there was no alternative. I prayed at her bedside while we waited for a doctor. Within minutes, a heart specialist appeared. He spoke with me, and it was clear by his questions that he thought the problem was with Rhoda's heart. He ordered a blood test, and minutes after that came back and told us that he was going to do an EKG because he didn't like what he saw in the blood test. Minutes later, a young man came in to do the EKG. I insisted that he tell me the results. He said that hospital policy stated that he couldn't tell me, and he ripped the printout from the machine and quickly left the room. I could tell by his urgency that something was seriously wrong. A few more minutes passed before the heart doctor came back to tell us that Rhoda had massive heart attack, and that "she's having another one right now!" He called in a code red, and Rhoda was transported to the Lancaster hospital. I rode in the ambulance with her along with two nurses. When we got to the hospital, Rhoda was taken into the operating room, where she had stents and a balloon put into her heart. The balloon expanded and contracted to make sure that Rhoda's heart was pumping. This allowed her heart to relax and stop going into spasms. The balloon was in her heart for four days. When the balloon was removed, we were relieved to see that Rhoda's heart was able to resume pumping. Our prayers had been answered.

There were a lot of prayers at her bedside during those four days from family, friends, and her minister. These were simple prayers and written prayers, but they were all from the heart, and I know they helped to save her life. The doctors told me after the balloon was removed that they couldn't believe Rhoda had survived such a serious heart attack. There was a nurse who came to see Rhoda who cried at her bedside and told Rhoda that she never expected to see her again. They all said, "It was a miracle." I truly believe that it was.

Rhoda was in intensive care for 11 days. Nobody knew if she would recover or not. I constantly prayed, but I came to terms with the possibility that

God might call Rhoda home. If that happened, Rhoda would be with her two daughters, Tara and Trisha, who had died at birth after full-term pregnancies. I found comfort in that because this was something that Rhoda often talked about. However, God gave Rhoda the strength to fight, and she recovered enough to go home. She wore a life vest to monitor her heart that would also shock her heart if it failed again. She also started physical therapy to help her regain her strength. There is no doubt in my mind that she had been very close to dying. Prayers, God's love, and a very talented medical team had saved her.

Over a seven-week period, I took Rhoda back and forth to physical therapy. At the end of the physical therapy treatments, a doctor's visit was scheduled. Before we went to see the doctor, we went to the local mall to buy thank-you cards for all the people who were so helpful and kind to Rhoda. While we were at the mall, I developed a pain in my chest. I thought this was unusually painful for indigestion, but I wasn't about to complain to someone who had just survived a massive heart attack, so I didn't mention this to Rhoda. During the short drive to Rhoda's doctor, my arms started to go numb, and the pain in my chest got worse. I knew something was drastically wrong with me. I still hadn't said anything to Rhoda because I didn't want to upset her, and I knew she couldn't drive because of the vest she was wearing. When we arrived at the doctor's office, Rhoda took the elevator, but I said I wanted to take the steps, thinking that the exertion would help relieve the indigestion. By the time I got to the top of the steps, my chest was really hurting. I walked into the doctor's office and went to where Rhoda was talking to some nurses. I leaned over and said to her, "I either have the worst case of indigestion or I'm having a heart attack." Seconds after I said that, I collapsed. I was having a heart attack, but fortunately I was at a place that could get me immediate help. I was quickly taken to the local hospital, which was only 10 blocks from the doctor's office. I recall thinking during this short trip that I was prepared to die. I was at total peace because I felt I was going to be with God. I was not afraid, even though I was in excruciating pain. That's very comforting during a time of great distress. That is a message from this book that is worth repeating—*you will be at peace in difficult times if you have a relationship with God!* I don't believe you can experience this peace without faith.

Four stents were put in my heart, which alleviated the pain. I was in the hospital for three days. The doctor told me that I had a heart attack for two reasons: the stress I was under from selling my business, and the terrible stress I experienced because of Rhoda's heart attack and my fear that she was going to die. She means everything to me. I can't imagine life without Rhoda.

For the most part, my heart was fine after the stents were inserted. Rhoda's heart had been badly damaged. Thirty percent of her heart was not functioning. We worked hard to restore our health, and soon after we were feeling better, we made another trip to New Zealand. The heart attacks made us realize how precious life is, so we decided we were going to live the life we wanted as best as we could and do as much as possible to help others. We decided it was time to apply for residency and find a place to live in New Zealand.

Moving to New Zealand

We were fortunate that we applied for residency when we did because I was within months of not being able to do this because of my age. I was 59 and the cutoff is age 60. There were many criteria that we had to meet to become residents, and amazingly we were able to meet all of them. I would estimate that there are close to 100 stipulations that are evaluated, such as education, work history, health, age, etc. We had to get physicals, go through criminal background checks and fingerprinting, and confirm sources of income. This was very difficult and time-consuming, and our attorney was concerned about our chances because of our age and the heart attacks we had. To help offset any deficiencies with any of the criteria, or to expedite the residency process, one can lend money to the country of New Zealand for four years. The lender has input on where they want the money invested, but other than that, the government controls the money. I recall that there were 12 activities approved by the New Zealand government that one could invest in. For example, you could invest in dairy farms, crop farming, hospitals, or a business. The investment pays interest, and the money is returned at the end of the four-year period. We decided to make this investment and get our residency. At the end of the four-year period, we will become citizens if we haven't broken any laws. Rhoda became a resident even though she spends the majority of her time in the United States. I am the primary applicant, and to maintain my residency, I have to spend at least three-quarters of the year in New Zealand.

After Rhoda and I attained residency, we concentrated on finding an area where I would live. In 2014, I settled on the town of Wanaka. I selected

Wanaka because of the size of the town. Wanaka has about 6,500 residents, which gives me everything I need without the hustle and bustle of a large city. The town is near the Southern Alps and is located on the south shore of Lake Wanaka. The area is breathtaking. There are many recreational activities in and around the town. It's an ideal town for someone who loves the outdoors, as I do. It is also a holiday town for residents of larger cities like Auckland, so Wanaka has a cosmopolitan feel to it. Wanaka is a 40-minute drive from Queenstown, a city of 15,700 people that swells to 27,000 during tourist season, with an airport and lots of arts and cultural activities. Rhoda and I love Wanaka and the lifestyle we enjoy there, and I plan to stay there for a long time.

I am a project guy. I must always have a project going to keep me busy. My first project in Wanaka was to find a home I could remodel, or "Mike it," as Rhoda likes to say. Rhoda is accustomed to my always having something under construction. I found my project house on Stone Street and started to rebuild the home. This was a nice property and home, but it needed a lot of renovations to make it to my tastes.

A big project turned into a huge project, which is normal for me. The project took two years, and I ended up putting a lot more money into it than I had planned. I was concerned about the amount of money that I had put into the house because a downturn in real estate could occur at any time. The property was now one of the most expensive in Wanaka, and that can be a problem when values are typically determined by the value of surrounding properties. I knew if I ever sold the house, I would have to find a buyer looking for a very unique property. Remodeling the house was always just a project for me, and it was not a home that I planned to live in for a long time. It was too big and impractical for one person, so I decided it was time to sell the house. My plan was to transition from an expensive house on a small piece of property to a modest house on a large plot of land. This is when I started to think about buying a farm.

During the time I was renovating the Stone Street property, I started to attend services at Saint Columba's Church, a 20-minute walk from my home. This is where I met Reverend Damon Plimmer, the vicar of three churches: Saint Columba's, the Tarras Church, and Saint Andrew's in the town of Cromwell. Damon was instrumental in introducing me to the Tarras Church, the focal point of my most recent Godly experience. He lives in Wanaka on the same block as Saint Columba's church. He is a dynamic man who lives a simple life in the service of God. Damon is in his midforties, and he is married to his beautiful and caring wife Raewyn. They have three children. Raewyn works for a charity and travels a few months during the year to help others in need. Damon is a special man who radiates his love for God. You feel that when you are around him. He is very active with his church congregation. He is a gifted speaker, and he preaches about topics that are contemporary and useful in everyday life. A mutual friend told me that Damon preached at the Tarras Church on the second Sunday of the month, which is the only Sunday that the church is open. I wanted to attend services where Damon was preaching. That is how I discovered the Tarras Church.

The Tarras Church

The church is a 40-minute drive from my home in Wanaka. It is situated on a four-acre plot of land and sits on a knob overlooking the beautiful New Zealand landscape. The property is surrounded by magnificent evergreen trees. It was opened in March of 1921. When I first went there I immediately knew there was something special about the Tarras Church. I knew in some way that I was going to be called upon to help the church even though I didn't yet understand how. After my first visit, I went to the church as often as I could. One Sunday I remember looking out the cut glass windows at snow falling on a day that you wouldn't expect it to snow. This view had a spiritual feel to it, like a photograph on a Christmas card. It was incredibly beautiful, and it got me to thinking about how I could make this church an important part of more people's lives. I also remember another Sunday when I sat in the church and was overwhelmed by the beautiful sound of birds singing. They were so loud I could hardly hear Damon speak. It was unbelievable to me how nature touched this beautiful church and how God was making me aware of what a special place it was.

As time went by, my friendship and respect for Damon grew stronger. I felt comfortable talking to him about spiritual matters, and I started to feel more connected to the two churches where I went to hear him preach. One Sunday at a service at the Tarras Church, Damon's sermon really hit home with me. He talked about something that I have talked about throughout this book—the question of, "Why me?" Why did God pick me to have experiences? When the service was over, Damon spent a few minutes speaking with the 8 to 10 people who were in attendance. After he was finished talking with them, he saw me standing in my pew and came to greet me. I was feeling troubled that day about "Why me," but I don't think it showed on my face. We talked briefly, and then I reminded him of some of the experiences that I had shared with him. I posed the questions—"Why me? Why sinners like me?" I told him this had always bothered me, and I asked him if he knew of others who had similar experiences. He looked into my eyes and said calmly and reassuringly, "I know why, Mike. It is for the same reasons the disciples asked Jesus why they were selected. They were common, seemingly undeserving people who had sinned, too. God calls ordinary and common people to do extraordinary things." I'm not calling myself a disciple, but Damon's explanation helped to answer my questions. I am one of those people who have been called to spread the message of God's grace.

Grace Farm New Zealand

More than two years had passed since I moved to New Zealand. I had bought and renovated a beautiful home, made many friends, and found a spiritual life in Wanaka and at the Tarras Church. I had not put my home on the market, but I made the decision that I was going to sell it, and the idea of buying a farm was becoming more appealing to me.

In late 2016, I made a trip to Pennsylvania to spend time with Rhoda and to see my family and friends. While I was in Ephrata, I spent time searching the Internet for farm properties that were close to Wanaka. One property looked very appealing to me, and I called the real estate agent to get some details. I was planning to fly back to New Zealand in a few days, so I arranged a time to meet with the real estate agent to see the property the day after I got back.

The moment I opened the door of the real estate agent's car and my foot hit the ground at the farm, I knew that this was going to be my new home. There was no doubt in my mind. It was the same feeling of confidence and excitement that I had when I first visited New Zealand. It was interesting to me that I did not have that feeling when I bought and remodeled the home I was now trying to sell. I stood next to the car and glanced at the panorama of the property. I took it all in, and within minutes I looked at the real estate agent and said, "I'll buy it!" He said, "I have three other properties to show you." I told him I didn't need to see them because I knew this was the land I wanted. It was five minutes from Wanaka. The gorgeous property was the size I was looking for. It was irrigated, with beautiful and healthy crops, and a magnificent 360-degree view.

After the real estate agent took me home, I thought about the commitment I had made to buy the property. Rhoda called that night, and I told her in casual conversation that I had bought a farm that day. Rhoda replied with a little bit of concern in her voice, "Are you serious?" I assured her that I was.

This was a substantial purchase, and all my money was tied up in my home and the money I invested for residency in New Zealand. I thought and prayed about this, and I became concerned that I could not pull this off. Then one night, it dawned on me that I might be able to get my money that was being held for four years for residency if I was investing in a working farm, not just a home. The idea came to me after praying about my dilemma. I thought this was worth investigating because it struck me as the kind of thing the government would encourage residents to do who had moved from another country to New Zealand. I could set up an income-producing operation on the farm that would contribute to the economy of the country. I called my immigration attorney, Mark Williams, in Auckland. Mark helped Rhoda and me get our residency, and he has been a huge help to us. Mark's first reaction was discouraging. He told me that to do this, my farm would have to meet many criteria, including the amount of land, which he didn't think was enough to qualify as a working farm. He was reluctant, but he agreed to look into it. Several days later, he called to tell me he was astonished to learn that we could meet every criterion that he was concerned about and that I could get my money back from the government to buy the farm. I would not only get back the money I had invested, but I would also get the interest the investment had accumulated. The total of my original investment plus the accumulated interest was the amount I needed to buy the farm. My prayers had been answered. God's grace had touched me again. I thought, *What a miracle.* Now I was able to buy the farm and still live in my house because I didn't need the cash from the sale of my home to buy the farm. I still wanted to sell the house and use the money to build a residence and other buildings on the farm, but the pressure to have to sell it quickly was removed.

I bought the farm from Ken and Jackie Roberts, who are two of the nicest people you could ever meet. They are members of the church I attend in Wanaka. Ken is a well-known and highly regarded farmer who is teaching me how to work my property.

He is a legend in and around Wanaka because of his farming skills. He has his hands full, but he is a determined, patient teacher, and I am a willing student.

Selling My Home

My next step was to hire a real estate agent to sell my home. As I expected, the agent found the house difficult to price. We decided to list it as a deadline sale where interested buyers would submit sealed bids within my 90-day contract period. We had three similar bids that were 25 percent less than I wanted, and I turned them down. I was becoming very concerned that I could not sell the property without taking a substantial loss on what I had invested in remodeling the home. I was worried, and I decided to do what I often do when I have a difficult problem or challenge. I turned it over to God. I "let go and let God!" When I let go, I stop worrying. I decided that if a sale was not to be, I would be okay with that. If the house sold, then God intended that to happen. This mind-set of letting go and trusting God to help me has served me very well throughout my life.

At the end of the 90-day contract period, I turned the listing over to another agent. Within two weeks, this new agent brought a man from Auckland to see my property. After some negotiation, we agreed on a price that was very close to what I wanted, and I sold the property. All the inside and outside furniture and the decorations in the house were new, and they were all part of the sale. When I left, all I had to take was my clothing. Selling my property this quickly, and for the money I received, surprised my real estate agent. I didn't get the exact amount I wanted, but I pictured God smiling and saying, "Mike, don't get greedy."

Life was good. I had my farm, I sold my house, and I had cash available to build at my farm. I was able to do this without any financial hardship to me and my family. I felt very fortunate and blessed, and I knew in my soul that this occurred because God wanted this for me. Then I found out that God had something else for me to do.

God's Message

Three weeks after I signed the agreement of sale on my house, I was taking my morning shower and saying my prayers as I always do. After I prayed, I was thinking about things in general, like how Rhoda and the kids and grandkids were doing. I wasn't thinking about anything specific like the farm I had just bought or the house I had just sold. When I do this, I often talk out loud to myself. While I was thinking and talking out loud, a message came into my mind where God revealed to me to "buy the Tarras Church!"

My first reaction was "no way." Even a small church like Tarras would cost more money than I could afford or want to pay. I thought, *Why would I even want to do that? I allocated all my money for the farm I just bought.* The instant I put my own interests first, I felt embarrassed and said to myself, *Now wait a minute, Mike, God has provided for you. You sold your business for the amount you wanted. You found New Zealand and were able to build and sell a beautiful home you really didn't need. The country of New Zealand returned your residency investment so you could buy and develop your farm. How could you even question why God wanted you to buy this church when God made the means for you to do this possible?* This was a wake-up call for me. I decided before I got out of the shower that I was going to help the Tarras Church. I didn't like the idea of "buying" a church because I felt that no one owns a church, but at first I thought that God wanted me to buy and own the church. I was thinking of buying and owning as one and the same. This weighed heavily on my heart. Then I realized that God had revealed to me to buy the church, and that meant to provide the funds, not actually put the church in my name and own the property like you would a home. I could have lost millions of dollars selling my business. I could have lost hundreds of thousands of dollars selling my home. New Zealand might have insisted on keeping the money I put up for residency and I could not have bought the farm. None of that happened. I was blessed that everything worked out for me. It would be very selfish of me not to help the Tarras Church. I realized that all of my good fortune and my ability to help the church were only possible because of God.

This Godly experience occurred on a Sunday morning. I went to church in Wanaka that day and spoke with my friend Fred, the retired judge. He was part of a group of people who were responsible for the operation of the Tarras Church. I said to Fred, "Don't ask me any questions because it's a long story, but I want to buy the Tarras Church." The church was for sale because the Presbyterian Church, the current owners, no longer used the church and wanted to sell it. The Tarras community was negotiating to purchase the church, and the process had been dragging on for some time. I explained to Fred, "God revealed to me this morning to buy the Tarras Church. I need to talk to the right people in order to get that done." Fred was excited, and he went to get Damon to involve him in the conversation. Damon told me that he was glad to hear this, and that he knew the price was significantly less than I had previously heard. This was great news and amazing to me because I was prepared to pay a higher price. Damon asked me not to speak to anyone else about this until he had a chance to talk to Felicity, the solicitor who handled the church's legal affairs.

Damon came to see me a few days later to update me on the conversations that were going on with the townspeople who wanted to keep the church operating. The Tarras community and I are currently in the process of finalizing our negotiation with the Presbyterian Church. It is intended that a charitable trust will be established to purchase and maintain the church. I will put money into the trust to buy the property. The end result will be that the church is debt free and has enough funds to operate for many years to come. It was important to me that the message from God is fulfilled—to buy the church.

By structuring the transaction this way, I felt I fulfilled my commitment to God to buy the church without ever owning it. This money will be used to maintain the church as a religious site. It will be available and open to all religions that believe in

God, not just Christians. I plan to be actively involved with the operation of the church. I expect that this will be another interesting chapter in my spiritual life.

This was the outcome of the message from God to buy the Tarras Church. It was a Godly experience, and a wonderful example of how God's grace is still touching my life today—a life of never-ending grace.

This book is about Godly experiences that have occurred since I was 17 years old. The experience you have just read about, starting with visiting New Zealand, then selling my business, and then moving here, is recent. My financial and personal involvement with the Tarras Church is now. God is still in my life right up to this moment and always will be. Just like the universe, there is no beginning and no end to God's love. God can and will be with you throughout your life if you have faith and put God first, and you can start that relationship at any age. There is no better time than now. Open your mind and open your heart, and let God's grace shine on you.

I don't think the experiences in this book are my final experiences. I expect to have more, and I hope that includes learning that this book has brought readers one step closer to God and to experiencing undeserved gifts and love.

Tarras Church, New Zealand, 2018

Tarras Church Christmas service, 2017

HISTORY OF THE TARRAS CHURCH

Opened 13 March 1921 by Rev. John Ryley

Situated on a four acre site, on a hill surrounded by a splendid selection of evergreen trees, the Tarras Church is a facility the community is proud of. The land was donated by Mr. R.K. Smith of Malvern Downs and his wife Elizabeth donated the bell. The documents of land entitlement are dated 6 May 1921.

The church was built by the Tarras people at the cost of 1900 pounds and as the times were difficult the Presbyterian Synod of Otago granted 900 pounds and the church was registered as a Presbyterian church in 1928.

Construction work was commenced in 1920, the church finally being declared open by Rev. John Ryley on 13 March 1921, when a large number of people assembled for the ceremony. The project was helped along by many generous gifts, the four acre site being donated by R.K. Smith, the bell being donated by Mrs. R.K. Smith, the organ by Mr. and Mrs. Roderick Polson and a communion service by Mr. Henderson of Tarras.

Prior to 1921 the Presbyterians and Anglicans had for many years held their services in the school, but the beginnings of the Presbyterian ministry in the district go back to 1864, when that remarkable man, Rev. Chas. Connor, became minister of St. Paul's in Oamaru and a parish of 3000 square miles which included the whole of Waitaki Valley, Upper Clutha and Maniototo. Leaving a neighboring minister to care for his home area, on at least four occasions beginning in 1861, Connor set off on horseback up the Waitaki Valley to cover the whole of the huge outlying parish, calling on all sheep stations including Morven Hills and conducting services and distributing tracts as he went. Connor, some fifteen years later, became the first school teacher in Pembroke.

Mike at the Rob Roy Glacier in New Zealand, 2016

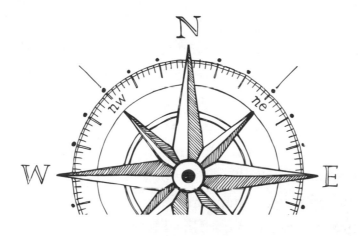

XVI.

Reflections

Writing this book has made me reflect on a number of things. I really do find it amazing that this book exists. I am a dyslexic, junior high school dropout, who failed the second and third grades. Now I can reflect on my experiences and think about the impact they have had on my life and the impact this book might have on others.

Putting and keeping God first is the most important and rewarding thing I have ever done. The second most important thing is trying to keep my spiritual compass pointed to the teachings of the Ten Commandments. That is followed by personally sharing my experiences with others and then writing this book, with the hope that both will help others find their way to God—to bring them one step closer to knowing God's grace.

I have a number of things that I can hold in my hands from my experiences in addition to this book. I have the Grace Friendship and Partnership Contract and the book *A Look at Life from a Deer Stand* by Steve Chapman that gave me the answer to how to resolve a conflict I had with my two sons. I have the handwritten note that a very spiritual homeless man gave me stating the number of days that had passed since the biblical flood began. There is also the skull from the bear that I killed with a miraculous shot, the site plan of my farm that shows the spot where I saw the Godly light, and the rosary beads that the medical technician gave me. Having something to hold that came from these experiences is very special to me.

At age 65, I have learned that I have a lot to learn. I make the commitment every day to live, learn, and pass it on, and to keep my spiritual compass pointed to the teachings of the Ten Commandments. This is often a struggle. At times, I lose my way and sin. I would like to say that I always learn from these mistakes, but sometimes I have not. When I fail, the only thing I know to do is ask for forgiveness, reset my compass, and try harder. With God's guidance, I have always been able to find my way back. God is always watching over us and helps us when we are spiritually lost. That's a lesson I have learned that we can all benefit from.

I have had these experiences over a 50-year period. Often, long periods of time would pass between them. As I look back, I can see that at first, the experiences were short in duration and impact, but as time passed, they lasted longer and had a much more powerful effect on me. This culminated with the creation of the Grace Friendship and Partnership Contract—the experience I call my Super Bowl. I often wonder if each experience was a test. If I passed the easier test, did God challenge me with another, more difficult test of my faith? I also wonder if my tests have ended, but I doubt it. God will always be with me.

I continue to wonder why I have been chosen to have these experiences. I am humbled that they have happened to me and truly believe that other people are more deserving. I have often faltered in my personal life. I have succumbed to temptation. I have tried, but sometimes I have fallen short of my goals. I have lived a life filled with success and failure. I would like to get past the "Why Me?" but I find this difficult to do. I believe that writing this book is another test. Is my faith strong enough to write a book about my sins and my spirituality—to let people know that God's love is available to all of us, even if we feel undeserving? If we have the courage to embrace faith and open our hearts and minds to all the possibilities, we can know God's grace.

I would be foolish to think that I am the only person who has experienced God's grace. I'm sure that some people have had more spiritual experiences than I have had, or experiences that lasted longer than mine did. Others may have had experiences that they think of as mere coincidences. I know there are people who are more capable than I to share their experiences with others. I hope this book encourages everyone to come forward and share them, regardless of how ordinary or extraordinary they think their experiences are. You don't need to write a book to do that. You can talk and think about God anywhere. I believe that simply loving God is an experience that we should be proud to talk about. Starting an open dialogue is something we should do.

You don't need to have an experience to know God's grace. God loves all of us whether we have had an experience or not. I have had experiences, and that makes it easy for me to believe, but that does not make me more special than someone who has not. People who believe based on faith alone are very special people. Having faith, without having a Godly experience, is the ultimate test of spirituality.

Each one of my experiences has taught me a lesson. I thought it was a curse when I had the accident in the Army and laid in a cast from my armpits to my toes for months. I now know that it was a blessing. I was kept still so I had the time to think about my personal life and my spiritual life. I believe that God was a part of me from the time I was born, but this time I spent in the cast thinking, especially about God, is when my spiritual journey took root.

I remember being driven to my knees for participating in the act of adultery when I was 19 years old like it happened yesterday. I can take you right to the spot where I was driven to my knees. I remember the feel of the grass and the brightness of the moon. I can still picture the view I had from the hilltop where I knelt. The location and overwhelming fear that gripped me are burned in my memory. My concept of a spiritual compass was something that I had been thinking about. That day, I did not follow my compass. My actions took me off course, and I broke one of the Ten Commandments. I learned at an early age that God is aware of the actions we take, right and wrong, in our lives. I wish I could say that this experience immediately changed my behavior, but it did not. What it did do was make me very aware of the presence of God in my life, and that God expects me to work hard every day at being a better person. I had sinned, and I was shown that this was wrong. I continue to pray that I will live the life that God intends for me to live, as free from sin as is humanly possible.

I owned and operated a successful business for 28 years. I give all the credit to God first, and then to my family, employees, and customers for my success. Many times in my business career I did not know how to solve a difficult problem the business was experiencing, and I would pray for guidance. Then I would wake up in the middle of the night with the answer. These were problems that might have destroyed the business. I know that God gave me the answers to my prayers. I didn't always like the answer, but I believed that God knew what was best for me.

I also know that God helped me to find the right people to run my business. I was blessed throughout my career to have outstanding employees. I also believe that God brought people to my business who needed help, and I hired them. Not every person worked out, but most did, and I am very thankful that I had the opportunity to make a difference in their lives. God has many ways to show us how to help others, and none are more powerful than to give people the opportunity to find meaning in their lives. Hiring people was a way for me to help. Being able to do that was a gift. It is an example of God's grace.

My wife, Rhoda, is the most important person in my life. Meeting her was a gift from God. My first marriage to a beautiful and wonderful woman lasted for 14 years. Her name was Patty. She will always be a special part of my life. It was my fault that our marriage did not work out. I was too consumed with my personal needs and ambitions. I was blessed to meet Rhoda several years after Patty and I separated. God helped me to see what changes I had to make to be a good husband. I needed to understand that there is a big difference between loving someone and being in love with someone. I had to put my marriage before my personal ambitions. You might find it strange that Rhoda and I live separately for a good part of the year. I know it's unusual, but Rhoda knows how happy I am living in New Zealand, and I know how important it is to her to live in Pennsylvania to be close to her family. It's the right thing for both of us at this time of our lives, and we make it work. We talk every day and share the ultimate love for God, each other, and our family. We are so spiritually connected that the distance and time apart only strengthen the bond between us. We do miss being with each other daily. If the time comes to change where we live, God will let us know. I talked earlier about my "love box." At the top of my love box is God, immediately followed by Rhoda. She is the only person who will ever occupy that place in my life. I will never be in love with another person like I am in love with Rhoda.

I know I would still be smoking today if it weren't for God. Once I asked for help to overcome my addiction to nicotine, I knew that I would stop because of my faith. God has always been there for me when I had a problem that was too difficult to solve on my own. It's not as easy as just asking for help. You must make an effort on your own to change, and you must follow through on your commitment to make the change. You must put God first in your life, and then you must believe that God will help you. You will be helped if you believe in God and you are committed to doing the hard work that comes with overcoming difficult problems. Answering our prayers for help is an example of God's grace.

I loved the experience of hunting. I loved preparing for a hunt. I loved practicing with my bow. I loved seeing the majestic places throughout

North America where I hunted. But, as I look back, I realize that I always hated the killing because it was mainly for sport. Every time I killed an animal, I would walk up to it with tears running down my face, kneel down, and pray. This started when I was a young boy, and I shot a sparrow with a BB gun. I always felt sorrow when I killed an animal. Halfway through my hunting career, I made a promise to God that I would have a taxidermist preserve as a life-size model any animal that I killed. I thought this commitment would reduce how much I hunted, or make me stop hunting, because I wouldn't life-size an animal that was not a premier example of the species and of trophy quality. That, and the significant cost to life-size an animal, would limit my hunting. Many animals were in my trophy room, and I would often sit alone with them with sadness in my heart. I started to wish that I could wave a magic wand and make all the animals come back to life. I believe this was God's way of letting me know that it was time to stop hunting. This inspired me to make another promise. I prayed that if I ever found some thing or some place that I enjoyed as much as hunting and being with nature, I would put away my bow and arrows and stop hunting. Soon after I made this promise, I traveled with Rhoda to New Zealand. The moment I touched the soil of New Zealand, I knew that I had found a magical place that would replace hunting in my life. I believe that God sent me there. When I came back to Pennsylvania, I affixed my bow to the top of the cathedral ceiling of my trophy room and never hunted again.

I am not condemning hunting. I have very fond memories of hunting. Many of my closest friends are hunters, and I'm happy that they still look forward to their hunting trips. Tom Hoffman, a close friend whom I love dearly, is a world-renowned archery hunter and I still love to hear his hunting stories. I don't preach to my friends that they should stop hunting. I made a promise that I would stop hunting if I found something that replaced the joy of being with nature, and I'm very thankful I found that in New Zealand.

The relationship between parents and their children is often very challenging. It certainly has been for me. I had a very difficult relationship with my father. I could be angry at him for not giving me the time, love, and encouragement I wanted, but I am convinced that my father did the best he could, and I love him more today than I ever did. I was blessed to have two wonderful parents who taught me, provided for me, loved me, and let me go when it was time for me to find my own way. I honor them as stated in the Ten Commandments, and I miss them deeply.

My two sons, Elton and Weston, might see similarities between our relationship and my relationship with my father. I haven't always been as present in their lives as I should have been. The decision to fire them for fighting at work the same week that my father passed away was one of the toughest decisions I ever had to make. It was "tough love" at the highest level, but love that was guided by wisdom and courage that God helped me to find. It is a perfect example of God answering my prayer: *God, give me the courage, the strength, the wisdom, and the ability to be a good Christian, to be a good husband, to be a good father, and to be a good employer.* I love my boys dearly, as much as a father could love his sons. I know that they are not perfect, none of us are, but I am very proud of the responsible adults they have become. I know that my boys love God, and that God loves them, and that God has had a positive impact on my relationship with them. I am thankful that they are such an important part of my life.

Knowing and helping the homeless was one of my most significant Godly experiences. It seems to me that I was always in the presence of the homeless, and always looking for ways to help the less fortunate. I wrote about my experience when I gave the homeless man a ride and I felt that I was in the presence of God or a messenger from God. This was the first time I felt God's presence next to me.

I tried to help other homeless men. A number of years ago I found a homeless man sleeping in his car. I gave him a furnished apartment in a building that was on the property of my Ephrata car wash. It didn't work out, but I felt I did the right thing by offering my help. It doesn't always work out when we try to help others, but we have to at least try. I think we should all lend a helping hand to the less fortunate through financial support or when we have the opportunity to personally help, like working in a soup kitchen. We can give our money or our time to those in need, and it's best if we can give both. I believe that I was being tested to see what I would do to help the homeless, but I also believe it was a lesson to let me know how bad decisions, or circumstances out of our control, can change our lives. Becoming homeless can happen to anyone. Knowing the homeless and helping the homeless gave me insight into my own life and my good fortune, and it gave me the wisdom and compassion to encourage others to help those who are in need. This is something the homeless gave to me, and it is just as meaningful as the help I gave to them.

I understand if you find my experiences in Chapter XI, Tests of Faith, including the writing of the Grace Friendship and Partnership Contract, fantastic or an exaggeration. If you have read this far, I hope that I have established credibility and trust. Everything in this book is accurate and true. I can't remember what I did yesterday, but I can vividly remember my Godly moments over a 50-year period. The experience surrounding the writing of the Grace contract was my most powerful experience for several reasons. The duration of time that passed lasted for a year and a half—from the time I met Roger, through the writing of the contract, my sickness, and arranging the financing that saved my business. During the night that the contract was created, I was in the presence of God for three hours. During this time, I was twice put in a childlike state and walked beside God. God guided my hand to write the contract. I recited prayers that I had never said before, and I saw the light of God come toward me and move away from me two times. These were the most beautiful and powerful moments that I have ever had. In addition, I was driven to my knees for the second time in my life. God also let me know that I had not given my soul for my father's soul, and I was shown a glimpse of Heaven. I value all of my experiences, but nothing has had more impact on me than the experiences I had the night the Grace Friendship and Partnership Contract was created. I hope that all the people who became a part of that experience were drawn closer to God. I hope their faith was made stronger. I know that mine has been. I also hope that you will believe that you can experience God's grace as I did.

Getting to know Sister Rosemary, Mother Anne, and the other Carmelite nuns was a gift from God. What a beautiful group of women they are. They make this world a much better place. I find it amazing that the nuns can live in a monastery and dedicate their lives to prayer and yet be so smart about the secular world. I believe this wisdom is because of God's presence in their lives. Knowing them has made my life richer and more spiritually fulfilling. Of all the people I have been around in my life, I feel that the nuns are the closest to God. I feel the presence of God when I am with the nuns, much more so than any other person I have talked to or have known.

I don't think that I would have lived through and understood my illness without love, support, and prayers from Rhoda, Sister Rosemary, Mother Anne and the Carmelite nuns, and many others. I credit their prayers with saving my life. I needed their support during that time. Sister Rosemary and Mother Anne also helped me to understand why I was chosen to have the experiences I have had. They explained to me how God often chooses seemingly undeserving people like me, sinners and those who are poorly educated, because they are willing to share their experiences with others. God's messengers can be the most unlikely people. I am very indebted to the Carmelite nuns, and they will forever be an important part of my life. I also want to thank the nuns for helping me to understand the spiritual experiences that I have had in my life.

I don't know why some people want to talk about their spiritual life when they are with me. I'd like to think they sense that God is present in my life and that I am someone they can openly talk to without being judged. I do believe that there are people who carry God's presence with them—some who live spiritual lives and some who do not. Maybe I am one of them. I don't know why anyone is picked to receive God's grace. I didn't feel I was worthy, but I decided to tell others about my experiences. I pray that I say the right things when people sense this presence in me and ask me questions. I do want to explain my feelings about living a spiritual life with the hope that I will encourage others to think about their spirituality.

God's reminders are all around us if we put God

first and we open our eyes, hearts, and minds to see them and then accept them as more than coincidences. I believe that all of these messages have a purpose. Certainly some spiritual things that occur in our lives are coincidences or even luck, but not all of them.

I spent a lot of time visiting churches in New Zealand during the many years before Rhoda and I became residents. I enjoyed driving around the South Island and visiting churches. I stopped at almost every church I passed. Some were large and in cities, and some were small and in rural areas, like the Tarras Church. It didn't matter what religion or denomination they were; I visited every church I could, and there are a lot of churches in New Zealand. I walked around the properties, studied the buildings, and just tried to get a general feeling for the church. Many of the churches were open when I visited. I went inside and walked around to look at the stained glass windows, and then I would sit in a pew to think and pray before I would leave.

The churches were always beautiful in their own unique way, and I thought about their history and what people had to go through to build these churches. If it was Sunday, I would often stay for the service so I could listen to the sermon. I always found my visits interesting and informative. What troubled me was how few people I saw at the churches other than on religious holidays when they were packed. God was in their lives then. Why not all the time? When I visited during the week, I rarely saw anyone, and regular Sunday services were poorly attended. A church that could seat 300 people had 30 people in attendance, and that ratio was very common. People were not attending church, and I wondered why.

I often found churches that were locked, and this disappointed me. I think churches should be open all the time to allow people to walk in and pray. I'm sure there were valid reasons why these churches were locked, but it bothered me that this was happening. I recalled what I said to my managers about my homeless friend Frank. I wanted them to leave the car wash open at night so Frank could have shelter and warmth if he wanted. If he stole something or broke something, we could replace it. I feel the same way about churches—the doors should always be open. If something is damaged or stolen, it can be replaced. I believe God does not want anyone to be locked out of a church.

The other thing I see with the few people who are attending church other than on holidays is that they are older. People under age 40 are not attending church. They have drifted away, even those who attended schools where religious studies were part of the curriculum. They are losing or have lost their faith. Something failed them as they became adults. I do believe they are searching for something, and I believe in my heart that it is God. Because they have not been attending church, any visit to a church is awkward and outside their comfort zone. They wonder where to sit, what to wear, and how to speak with other people in the congregation. They wonder how to worship. This keeps them away.

When I encourage younger friends to attend Sunday service, I worry that they will be turned off because there is no one in church they can relate to. Their peers are not going to church. They have no one to talk to about their spiritual experiences. Young people are not talking to each other about the value of church and the role that God plays in their lives. I am committed to finding a way to show younger people a path to the glory of God and God's grace. Maybe this is what God has planned for me. Maybe this is my next challenge. People around the world are drifting away from God and the church, and worse, not getting any spiritual exposure as children and teenagers. I plan to do what I can to reverse this trend through my involvement with the Tarras Church. I also think that Grace Farm will play a role in this. I will pray to God for the courage, strength, wisdom, and ability to help young people find faith and to know God. I know this will be a challenge.

I have asked God a lot of questions. Why is there so much hunger in the world? Why do people do violent things? Why are there so many divorces? Why are there diseases, and why do children die, to name just a few? We are humans living on Earth, and it is not a perfect world. If life were perfect, we would be in Heaven, and life on Earth is not Heaven. I don't know what the criteria are for getting into Heaven, but I do believe there are things that we can do that enhance our chances. Heaven is our reward if we put God first, embrace faith, and believe even when we experience pain and suffering. I think this is the case, regardless of what religion or faith you practice.

I often wonder what people do when God is not in their lives and they are confronted with a tragedy, pain and suffering, or a conflict that must be resolved. In difficult times, I pray. Through prayer, I ask for help. Without the power of prayer, we lose our connection to God's grace. In 2014, I had a heart attack. An ambulance took me to the hospital, and during the ride it crossed my mind that I might die. My faith and my prayers put me at peace. I was relaxed and not afraid, and I was ready to die if God was calling me. I believe that all of us in a similar situation would want someone who had a relationship with God to pray for us. We want someone to pray, not just say, "I hope that you'll get better," or "I hope that you'll be okay." Non-believers can only hope, and hope is hollow when it is not supported by faith. Even if the outcome is negative, having a relationship with God gives us someone to talk to for support. I am very thankful that I believe in the power of prayer. Prayer can change lives. It has changed mine.

I have been blessed, and I have definitely known God's grace. I do want to make it clear that not all my prayers have been answered. Someday I hope to understand why some prayers are answered and some are not, but I accept it when God does not answer my prayers. I believe that all prayers are heard, but not all prayers are answered the way we want them to be. I believe that God has a reason for not answering all of our prayers. I believe that God knows what is best for us, even if we don't understand it.

I think about how we acknowledge God when we say "Thank God" when there is a positive outcome to something challenging in our lives. When we experience pleasure, we often say, "Oh my God, that's great." Saying "God" often means the best outcome has occurred. We use God to represent something good. If we give thanks frequently, and not just when we are pleased about something, we will find that God's grace will touch our lives in ways we didn't ask for or expect.

What if I'm wrong about God? What if there is no God? What if I have spent the better part of my life praying to and talking to a God who is not there? I think about that on occasion, and I have concluded what's the harm in that? I also think about what if there is a God and you don't believe? What happens then? I don't know, but my faith has made me feel secure about a life after death, and if there is no God, I have at least been a better person. My faith has given me God, my friend, whom I love and who I know loves me. It has given me a spiritually rich and fulfilling life. I can't imagine my life without God.

I have friends who don't believe. We talk openly about my faith and what it means to me. What I share with them is that believing has given me purpose and a sense of direction. I have felt this way since I was mature enough to understand that faith means choosing to believe in something you can't see or prove. There is not a specific moment that I can recall when I felt I found God. I feel that God was always in my life, as I believe God is in all our lives, and I recognized and accepted that at an early age. That's how it happened for me, but what's important is that you make God a part of your life, regardless of your age. I have met many people who accepted God later in their lives. It was through God's grace that I had these experiences. They would not have happened to me if I did not have the faith to believe.

This book is about spirituality. I think of myself as a spiritual person because I do more than go through the motions of religion. I am connected to God. I don't believe I've had these experiences because I go to church or know some scripture from the Bible. I do believe that church is important because it puts you in a spiritual atmosphere and helps you to set your compass and think about God. I encourage you to find a church and to be faithful to that church. I've had these experiences not just because I attend church, but because I put God first in my life. This has tested my faith a number of times, and I believe that writing this book is another test. God wanted me to find the courage, strength, wisdom, and ability to see this through. Would I open myself up to criticism by sharing my beliefs and experiences with others? I pray that I have passed the test.

I have said that this is not my book; this is God's

book. I prayed every day that I would get this right, to honestly and accurately tell you about my experiences. I prayed that my co-writer, Bob Ruhe, could capture my thoughts and memories in a way that was interesting to the reader. Bob and I did not spend a lot of time over the years discussing our spiritual beliefs. I am amazed at how the words on these pages capture what I think and how I feel. My prayers were answered.

I hope that this book has been spiritually thought-provoking. I don't have the answers to the mysteries of God, but I pray that I got you to think about your spiritual life and God's place in your life. I pray that this book has brought you one step closer to God. I put God first above everything else. God is at the top of my love box, and that makes it easier for me to empty my hate box. That is the foundation of my spirituality. Maybe you will decide to do the same, or at least make God a more important part of your life. Faith is the first step to experiencing grace—God's undeserved gifts and love.

Mike at Grace Farm New Zealand, in memory of his buddy Runner

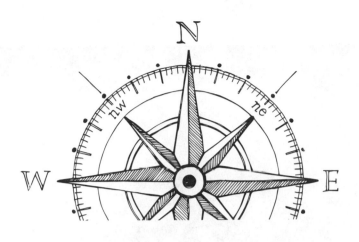

Final Thoughts

Believe in the power of faith. Believe in yourself. Be at peace. Love and be loved. Ask for forgiveness. Forgive yourself and forgive others. Live, learn, and pass it on. Try to keep your spiritual compass pointing true north. Consider putting and keeping God first in your life.

Cheers,
Mike Mountz

Lake Wanaka, Wanaka, New Zealand

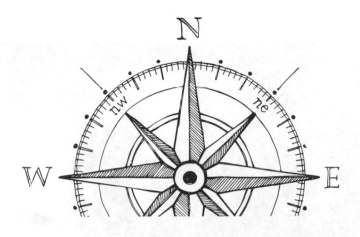

Acknowledgments

In addition to Rhoda Mountz, Bob Ruhe, and Jaime Markle, thank you to the following for their help in making the Godly experiences of a dyslexic man a book: Ralf Alphberg, Warren Bechtel, Lennart Bluemel, Dale Bowie, Thailand Cooke, Olivia Czeschka, Jaime Gallagher, Jan and Bern Healy, Paulette Kish, Ron Linder, Joan Nolan, Ralph Seidenstricker, Yarden Shamir, and Paula, Johannes, and Lucas Vollbehr, for their help with proofreading and editing; Sister Anne Brackman and the Carmelite nuns of Terre Haute, Indiana, for clarifying my memories of the time I spent with them; and Winton Davies, Randy Fox, Ned Pelger, and Damon Plimmer, for their general and valuable input. Thanks to the team at Momosa Publishing, Jennifer Bright Reich, Leanne Coppola, Joanna Williams, and Amy Kovalski.

Mike and Runner, New Zealand, 2015

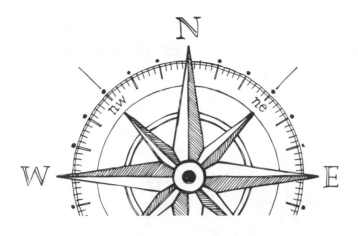

About the Author

Mike Mountz was born in Lancaster, Pennsylvania, on December 22, 1952. He has an older sister, Linda, and he was the second and last child of Elton and Lelia Mountz.

Mike did poorly in school, failing the second and third grades. He recalls being taken to a doctor after he failed both grades to find out if he had a learning disability. Mike was evaluated, but the doctor didn't know what was wrong. "He is not stupid" was the only diagnosis he could offer Mike's anxious mother. It was eventually determined that Mike was severely dyslexic, a condition that makes reading and writing difficult for Mike and a condition that was unknown during his early school years. Mike was reluctant and embarrassed to read out loud because he feared bringing attention to himself. Retaining what he tried to read was always a challenge. People with dyslexia have trouble with spelling and grammar and mix up words that sound similar. Reciting the alphabet is impossible for Mike. Living with dyslexia is incredibly frustrating, but it is something that Mike has worked hard to overcome.

Mike dropped out of school in the ninth grade and went to work in his family's business, Morgan Trailer Manufacturing Company, which was started by Mike's father and mother as a welding shop. Today it is known as Morgan Corporation, and it is the largest truck body manufacturing company in the world (www.morgancorp.com).

Elton and Lelia Mountz were successful business-people. Mike often had a difficult relationship with his father, who passed away in 2002. Mike credits his father for instilling in him the entrepreneurial spirit that served him well in business. Mike knows his father loved him; he just had a difficult time expressing his love or admiration for what Mike accomplished. He would tell others how proud he was of his son—he just never told Mike. Mike's mother, Lelia, was the driving force who taught him the importance of loving your family, caring for others, and living a meaningful and fulfilling life.

Mike worked at Morgan until he enlisted in the Army in 1969 at the age of 17. This was during the time of the Vietnam War. He was in the service for two years but was not sent to Vietnam. One night he fell out of a bunk bed and broke his pelvis, an incident that decades later led to the creation of Grace For Vets. The full story of Grace For Vets can be found at www.graceforvets.org.

When Mike got out of the service, he married Patty Jackson and started a family. They were married for 14 years. He went back to work for the family business, but he seriously started to think about owning his own company. Mike's goal was to own a company by his 30th birthday. He left Morgan at age 28, and three years later, he bought a small car wash in Ephrata, Pennsylvania, that employed one person, Del Burkholder, who worked with Mike until he sold the company. He owned and operated Cloister Car Wash for 28 years. In 2012, he sold the business to Mister Car Wash www.mistercarwash.com. The history of Mike's ownership of Cloister can be found by visiting www.cloistercarwash.org.

Throughout his life, Mike has battled the dual challenges of dyslexia and bipolar disorder (formerly known as manic-depression). He thinks managing his dyslexia helped him develop the skill of visualization. (Creative abilities, original insights, and "big picture" skills are often strengths of people with dyslexia.) Recognizing the rhythm of bipolar disorder made him focus on using his "up" time most productively. His ability to visualize was a big reason Mike was able to design and build car washes with innovations that are now used worldwide. To help others deal with dyslexia, he started *dad*, which stands for Dyslexics Achieve Distinction. *dad* is spelled with small letters because Mike could not distinguish between a small b and a small d. Mike likes to say he has a 50 percent chance of getting that right. For more information on *dad*, visit www.cloistercarwash.org under the community service tab.

After selling his business, Mike moved to Wanaka, New Zealand. He and his wife, Rhoda, were married in 1991. They split time between their farm in New Zealand and their home in Lancaster County, Pennsylvania. They have three children: Elton, Tonya, and Weston, and 12 grandchildren.

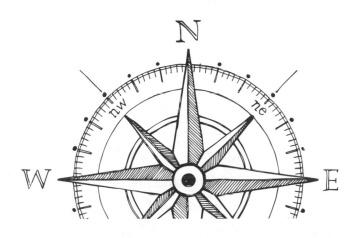

About the Co-Writer

Bob Ruhe and Mike Mountz met in 1975 when they worked at Morgan Trailer Manufacturing, a company founded by Mike's parents. From 1985 until 1990, Bob's advertising agency did work for Mike's business, Cloister Car Wash. Over the next two decades, Bob twice served as interim director of marketing for Cloister and has assisted Mike in the management of Grace For Vets, an organization that Mike founded. During his career, Bob was a senior-level executive and currently works as a training instructor and an adjunct professor of business. In 2000, Bob wrote *Letters to Heather*, a book that was featured on the *Oprah Winfrey Show*. Co-writing *Why Me? One Man's Journey Experiencing God's Undeserved Gifts and Love* has been the most profound creative experience of Bob's life. The 20-month project made Bob think about God and faith more than he ever had before. "I learned how important faith and spirituality are to Mike and other people, and how believing in God can lead to a more fulfilling life. I understood for the first time the concept of God's grace and how grace can touch anyone's life. Mike's book is a must-read for those interested in spirituality or people looking to discover or re-energize their faith."

Bob Ruhe touring New Zealand with Mike, 2010

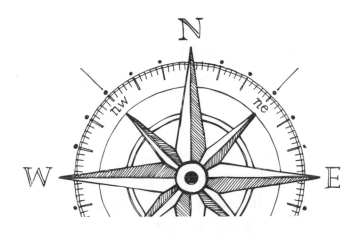

About the Co-Designer

Jaime Markle is a 2005 graduate of Kutztown University in Communication Design. She met Mike Mountz in 2010 when she was hired as a marketing specialist at Cloister Car Wash. They worked closely together on marketing efforts for the company until the sale of the wash in late 2012. After the sale, she focused on opening her own marketing and design business, On the Mark Studio. One client included Grace For Vets, an organization that Mike founded. They were able to continue working together on expanding the Grace For Vets initiative of providing free car washes to veterans on Veterans Day. During her career, she has worked in many fields ranging from retail to roofing, to car washes and veterinary medicine. As an avid animal lover, she volunteers her time and skills to help local animal shelters and rescues. When Mike asked for her help with the book's design, she was a little wary, as she's not the most spiritual person. To really understand the book, she had to read it multiple times to be able to visually portray what Mike's words were saying. The project has heightened her senses, allowing her to open her mind and heart to be able to accept spiritual guidance.

Jaime Markle with two of her beloved dogs in Pennsylvania

*Sister Rosemary at the Carmelite
Monastery, Terre Haute, Indiana*

In Memory

*This book is in memory of Sister Rosemary,
a Carmelite nun, who was called to God on
June 2, 2013. She was a huge influence on
my life, my spiritual mentor, and my dear
friend. She is deeply missed.*